PRAISE FOR
Succcessful Women, Angry Men

"Engrossing."

—*The Chattanooga Times*

"Valid . . . Campbell strongly believes that if both men and women make the effort, things can be worked out."

—*The Columbia (SC) State*

"Tackles a new problem facing career women."

—*Today's Chicago Woman*

"A good guidebook . . . Campbell recognizes the difficulty of dual-career marriages."

—*The Tampa Tribune & Times*

SUCCESSFUL WOMEN ANGRY MEN

Bebe Moore Campbell

BERKLEY BOOKS, NEW YORK

Grateful acknowledgment is made to the following for permission to reprint previously published material:

Essence Communications, Inc.; excerpts from the following articles printed in *Essence*: "Men Need Tenderness Too," by Martin Simmons, November 1982; "Why Married Women Take Lovers," by Wista Johnson, June 1984; "When Your Career Collides with Your Man's Ego," by Lenore Jenkins-Abramson and Elaine Ray, March 1982; and "You New Women Want It All," by Donald Singletary, July 1985. Copyright © 1982, 1984, 1985 by Essence Communications, Inc. Reprinted by permission.

The Philadelphia Inquirer: "Letter to the Editor," by Virginia M. DeGrazia, in *The Philadelphia Inquirer*, April 15, 1986. Reprinted by permission of *The Philadelphia Inquirer* and the author.

SUCCESSFUL WOMEN, ANGRY MEN

A Berkley Book / published by arrangement with
Random House, Inc.

PRINTING HISTORY
Random House edition / January 1987
Jove mass-market edition / February 1989
Berkley revised trade paperback edition / December 2000

The Penguin Putnam Inc. World Wide Web site address is
http://www.penguinputnam.com

ISBN: 0-425-17663-0

BERKLEY®
Berkley Books are published by The Berkley Publishing Group,
a division of Penguin Putnam Inc.,
375 Hudson Street, New York, New York 10014.
BERKLEY and the "B" design
are trademarks belonging to Penguin Putnam Inc.

PRINTED IN THE UNITED STATES OF AMERICA

10 9 8 7 6 5 4 3 2 1

Dedication

To my mother, DORIS C. MOORE, for her encouragement and inspiration throughout the years. To my husband, ELLIS GORDON, JR., for his love and support. And to my daughter, MAIA, and son, ELLIS III.

Acknowledgments

This book would not have been possible without the assistance of many special people. I would like to thank Wendy Reid Crisp, editor of *Savvy* magazine, for publishing the article that was the genesis of this book. Her wholehearted support and enthusiasm and her decision to make my article a cover story convinced me to make backlash the topic of a book. I want to thank Susan Taylor and the wonderful women of *Essence,* for allowing me the opportunity to grow as a writer over the years and develop the self-confidence I needed to write this book. Darlene Hayes was pivotal in helping this subject get national exposure. Charlotte Leon Mayerson and Leslie Gelbman provided the guidance needed to complete this project. Their expert judgment and critical analysis were invaluable and were an education for this writer.

I'm fortunate to have friends who know the meaning of friendship. I'm extremely grateful to Patrice Johnson, whose research and word-processing skills made this project a much easier one. And I appreciate all the help others extended as I interviewed men and women across the country. Special thanks to Judi Moore Latta, Roslyn Watson, Rita Louard, M.D., Edith Hammond, Jonelle Procope, and Francine and Marvin Greer.

Finally, I am grateful to the wonderful men and women who allowed me to come into their lives and share their stories. Without their trust, faith and candor, this book would not be possible. I hope that the work I've done will enable men and women to come closer together, bonded by friendship and a real desire to improve their lives.

Contents

ix

Contents

PART THREE
Working On It

Introduction

Successful Women, Angry Men
by Bebe Moore Campbell

T he wedding was beautiful: radiant bride, handsome groom, proud parents—extremely proud parents . . . and with good reason. Not only were the newlyweds attractive, but each one possessed that most emblematic of American talismans: a Harvard law degree. They both worked at prestigious firms and brought home the kind of paychecks that were made for platinum plastic overdrive. The mother of the bride was my friend. Months before she had shared with me her joy when Babygirl became engaged. To her credit, in describing her future son-in-law, she spoke of his character as well as his credentials. But it was undeniable that the thought of the combined beauty, brilliance, and earning capacity of her daughter and Mr. Righteous sent her over the edge of delirious mother-of-the-bride happiness. Still, my friend's euphoria was short-lived and tempered by the pragmatism gleaned from her own quarter of a century marriage. She too was a professional, married to a man who had uppercase letters following his name. She knew better than most that combining two lives and two careers demands stamina, dedication, perseverance, and dictates living in a constant state of compromise. So, my friend was far more reflective than jubilant: thinking, perhaps, of her own marital struggles; wondering, perhaps, if her daughter and her fiancé were more prepared for the challenges that awaited them than she and her own husband had been.

Nearly twenty years after the original publication of *Successful Women, Angry Men*, the concept of the two-career marriage is no longer new for most Americans. From James Carvelle and Mary Maitlin to Will Smith and Jada Pinkett to the doctor and dentist who enjoy one marriage and two shingles, professional couples have become the rule and not the exception. Most couples who say "I do" today acknowledge that for the majority of their married lives each will be employed outside of the home, and that when children are born, the wives will become working mothers. The question is no longer whether both husband and wife will have careers but how well they can manage marriage and professions. Like my friend's daughter and her betrothed, adults who came of age in the nineties more than likely have been parented by working mothers and fathers. But if baby boomers have carved out a path for their offspring to follow, they haven't cleared that road of marital land mines. The same issues that plagued the first crop of dual professional households are confronting yet another generation, and these problems are exacerbated when children are born. Who picks up the kids? Who cleans the house? Do we move across country for a job opportunity for him when she's doing great at her company? And what do we do if her dream comes true before his?

The current crop of young twenty-something newlyweds are far better equipped than I was when I made my first trek down the road of matrimony with the ink still wet on my college degree and my ambitions not yet conceived. I was a child of divorce, reared by a professional mother and a stay-at-home grandmother during the school year, and a paraplegic father and his mother during the summers. Other than people I babysat for during my teenage years, the uncles and aunts I saw sporadically, the Ricardos, and the Cleavers, I had no idea how a traditional marriage worked, let alone one formed by two independent professionals seeking love and career satisfaction. My first husband and I weren't alone in the confusion, disappointment, and anger that tore our marriage apart. Like us, our peers were grappling with the question that all of us were afraid to answer: Who comes first in a marriage of equals?

America in the new millennium has made many strides toward equalizing the work lives of men and women. There are far more females represented in every profession than there were twenty years ago. The woman boss is not uncommon in many industries. While there is still a need for good, affordable day care, improvements have been made with some forward-thinking companies instituting on-site day care centers.

But culture is harder to penetrate than commerce. Although in films and on television there are heroes who save the guy or at least help to save themselves, America is still a nation where men are ensconced firmly at the helm. This patriarchal society adheres to the credo that husbands are the heads of their houses and marriages, and asserts that males are the major breadwinners and wives the subordinate partners. And for all the progress the United States has made in affording equal opportunity to all its citizens, by and large, males still earn more than women.

When I wrote *Successful Women, Angry Men*, the problems of the two-career couple were hidden from view. Something was going wrong behind the closed doors of newlyweds with white-collar jobs, but nobody could name the problem. To be sure, women complained of being swamped with housework, of men who'd promised to help out with the children but failed to do so, of there never being time to talk about their work problems. And men raged about constant fast-food dinners, women who were always too tired for sex, and a vaguely uneasy feeling that they weren't getting the respect from their wives that their fathers took for granted. *Backlash* is what I termed the anger some husbands were feeling and acting out in the face of their wives' career success and abandonment of the traditional female role.

That anger still threatens to destroy marriages. The rage hasn't disappeared. With the onslaught of radio and television talk shows, the topic of how to manage a marriage of equals is now out in the open. But just because more people are talking about their marital pain doesn't mean they know how to end it. Far too many husbands and wives, who are juggling marriage, careers, and childcare, are too tired to recognize the symptoms of backlash, an all too common and pervasive malady. They know that their marriages don't provide the mutual support they expected, but they are out of touch with how to change their relationships. Overworked and hassled, they are too tired to analyze the symptoms of what's gone wrong, and they feel powerless to recharge their marriages.

I knew that I was covering new ground when I wrote *Successful Women, Angry Men*. As I traveled around the country in the mid-eighties, interviewing married couples in their twenties and thirties, the stories I heard of male anger in the face of female self-actualization didn't surprise me. My own experience, and those of many of my friends, had prepared me for what I perceived was a national problem. What did give me hope was the number of marriages that were without backlash, where two-career couples supported each other emotionally and professionally, where friendship was the building block to marital and career success. I assumed that by the millennium these partnerships would be the rule and not the exception, as New Age men and women relinquished the gender-based stereotypes of a bygone era and embraced the kind of equality that would enable both husbands and wives to soar.

Maybe next century. Recently I wrote an article about

issues in marriage for *Essence* magazine. I interviewed a young childless couple in their twenties. Recently married, the two New Yorkers were still in the euphoric, passionate stage of wedlock. Whiling away a Saturday in bed was the norm. Kissing for hours hadn't lost its thrill. Yet, when the wife described their fights, the issues were the same ones that my interviewees had been grappling with twenty years earlier. She reported that he had reneged on his promise to do his share of the housework. The young bride became enraged every time her husband failed to clean the bathroom, which was "his job." "I work just as hard as he does," she said. "It's not fair to expect me to do everything around the house."

The interviews included in this book are the original ones but make no mistake, they are still relevant for today's younger married couples—and for many older ones as well. The truth is young twenty-somethings can draw parallels from the issues outlined by the couples speaking in these pages. The generation may be different but the problems remain the same. And the prescription is still useful.

Successful Women, Angry Men is a cautionary tale. I mean it to be that word to the wise that will empower the reader to be able to recognize the symptoms of backlash before it undermines the relationship. Anger is a corrosive force with the power to destroy. The rate of divorce for Americans is the highest in the world. The results are even more destructive when children are involved. Today more than ever, two-career marriages need guidance. Successful women aren't going to disappear. If anything, their numbers are growing stronger in medical, business, and law schools across the nation, and in the highest echelons of corporate America. With increased participation comes the expectation that married women can juggle careers, marriage, and parenting without breaking a sweat, the presumption that if so many people are doing it, all must be well. Today young married women have even more pressure to succeed in both endeavors than did previous generations. Successful women and men have every right to achieve personal fulfillment as well as professional satisfaction. They can have both when husbands and wives know the pitfalls of combining two careers under one roof and ways to solve some of the problems that accompany two hefty paychecks, and two sets of long hours. This book provides a road-tested map that will help guide couples through the maze of difficulties. I offer it with the prayer that a new generation will learn from the old and serve as a beacon of hope to the next.

PART ONE

The New Marriage

The Two-Career Couple: Who Comes First in a Marriage of Equals?

I t was the wrong time for a visit that spring day in 1978. I'd driven to Philadelphia from Washington, D.C., earlier the same day, compelled by nostalgia, homesickness, and most of all the need to retreat from the seething anger that had been plaguing my marriage, making my husband and me two fierce warriors, each pledged to show the other no mercy. I was tired of fighting. I wanted my mom, my aunts and uncles, my high-school buddies. I wanted to be in my old neighborhood, wanted to walk down those oak-lined Germantown streets with the odor of hoagies wafting through the air. I wanted to go home, where I was loved, unconditionally loved. I wanted some peace and good times.

And that meant stopping by my old friend Gloria's house, for a slow cup of coffee and plenty of languid breeze shooting. We would pull out the old photo albums, the yearbook, and sift through all the good times. There would be lots of laughs, if her husband was there. My memories of Ben were of a clown, a delightful, irreverent clown.

Only, he wasn't being funny that day. I could hear him and Gloria not being funny as my raised hand was poised to ring the doorbell of their town house. I heard their voices: my girlfriend's usually well-modulated tones were screeches of high-pitched exasperation, jagged yelps of anger, tinged with hysteria. Ben hurled shouts of fury that slammed down venomously on the thick, heavy air surrounding them. "Bitch," I heard distinctly. Whoa. It was a fast, vicious fight. Ben and Gloria argued with clear and articulate vengeance; their ravings pierced through the quiet good taste of their grass-clothed walls, jarring the serenity of their tree-lined, refurbished urban neighborhood.

Ben shouted and accused. "I come home tired. I've been working all day and you can't even get a meal on the table. I'm tired of eating at ten o'clock every damn night."

Gloria denied and defended. "I work just as hard as you do. You never help me anymore."

"That's your job," Ben retorted.

It was wild, an intensely ugly moment, a private moment no outsider should have witnessed. Propriety commanded me to turn on my jogging shoes and leave. I shouldn't be hearing all of this, I recall thinking. My sudden, automatic response was a thunderbolt of truth, riveting me to the spot: But I have heard all this before.

4

It was all too familiar, this battle of the sexes, this domestic powerplay. Hadn't I zoomed up 95N to escape the very same scenario? Theirs wasn't a Lucy and Ricky Ricardo spat. The frenzy behind Gloria's closed doors was the kind of row that only a working couple could get into. I didn't know it then, but what I was running away from, what I was running into, was the domestic fight of the seventies and eighties. Ben and Gloria, an accountant and a lawyer respectively, were arguing about who would keep the house and the children, who could walk away from the mess in the kitchen and fall asleep on the sofa and who had to stay and clean it up, who would be first and who would come second in a marriage of equals.

Ben and Gloria hadn't begun their marriage fighting. Gloria had discussed with me how she'd told Ben about her professional ambitions. "I want you to know my career is really important to me," she'd said. "I don't want to have a baby until after I'm set in my profession. Whenever we do have a child, both of us should be equally responsible for the baby's care. And, of course, I believe men and women should split the household chores down the middle." Ben had responded as she'd hoped he would. It was okay by him for her to go on to law school. They could have a baby whenever she said the word. And he didn't mind doing his share of the housework. Or at least that's what Gloria told me. What Gloria had wrenched from the women's movement was the belief that her life could be different from her mother's. She would not have to ask her husband's permission to be who she wanted to be. No man would dump the kids and the house on her, while he went off in search of his rainbow. Ben's promise, she thought, delivered her from such a fate. With his support she could achieve as much as any man. In her euphoria, she failed to realize how difficult it would be for Ben to keep his promise and how impossible for her if he broke it.

There on the doorstep, listening to the barrage of accusations and denials, I felt enveloped in a harsh, wounding cocoon of déjà vu. Yes, I'd been there before and knew intimately the struggles involved in the metamorphosis of an egalitarian relationship; I was familiar with the wavy rhythms of marital discord that were rippling behind the brick wall that I faced. I knew all about unkept promises. Those were my problems, my secret problems being dissected behind someone else's closed door. My frustrations were seeping through the cracks of the window in screaming spurts. Those were my feelings coming out of another woman's mouth.

"You were the one who wanted to have a baby so badly," Gloria screamed. "You were the one who couldn't wait. You knew, you know that I'm trying to make partner. You promised that you'd help me with her, that you'd change diapers, feed her, bathe her, do everything that I do. You never help me."

I saw Gloria's point clearly, of course. How could I not? It was my own. If Ben had been trying to make partner, he would have expected Gloria to make sacrifices. He couldn't cope with the shoe being on the other foot. None of you men can, I wanted to yell.

Because I wasn't Gloria and I wasn't married to Ben, I forced myself to keep silent and to acknowledge that there was another side of the story. Ben's rage, his feelings of betrayal were as real to him as Gloria's were to her, mine to me. When I heard him say, "Why the hell do you need so much help? I'll tell you why: because you spend so much time at that damn job," I had to wince at some of the truth in his words. Gloria was very ambitious and she did work a lot.

"I'm sick of you being too tired to cook, too tired to change the baby's diaper, too tired for sex," Ben continued. "You're never too tired for that damn job. The job gets all your energy and you ignore your family. You don't care about being a wife to me or a decent mother; all you care about is making partner. And then what? You'll be too high and mighty to be bothered with us commoners, just like that jerk of a boss you have. Well, what about this partner? What about me? What about what I want from you? Huh? Huh? When I get what I want around here, maybe then you'll get some help."

I listened to Ben's words, to the man's side, as I had never listened before; and I had heard it before. Was what he was saying true? Was Gloria abandoning her role of wife and mother in favor of professional laurels? Was she emotionally and sexually neglecting her man because she found more pleasure in professional fulfillment? More important, was that what Ben really felt? Whenever I'd heard those accusations before, I'd always dismissed them as the wild rantings of an angry husband. Listening to Ben, I wasn't so sure his words didn't contain some merit. Behind his rage, there seemed to be genuine pain. I'd always thought that women were the victims. Ben was saying that he felt oppressed by Gloria.

"Before the baby . . ." Gloria began loudly, but her words were cut off by the slamming of a door. Ask me about before the baby, I thought to myself. Yes, before the baby there had been sharing and equality and time for making dinner, for making love. Before the baby there had been the apartment that would sparkle from a monthly swipe with a damp paper towel. Whose turn to put the two plates, two forks, and two cups into the dishwasher? Eenie, meenie, miney, moe. Back before the baby came, there was even time for sharing dreams of setting the world on fire from two respective offices. Before the baby, equality was, well it was kind of cute. Now there was a big house in a residential neighborhood and there was a baby inside and two adults who fought about who would vacuum and who'd broken the promise.

Gloria and Ben's voices became loud and strident again. They immersed themselves in a steady stream of verbal tit for tat until the persistent squawling of the baby signaled the downside of the fight. "Why don't you get her sometimes?" Gloria hissed. "You're her mother," came the retort—hard, sullen, and with an air of finality. I heard the staccato stamp of high heels going off into the back of the house to the baby's room. Almost immediately, the automatic garage door flew open and a sleek, compact car barreled out of the driveway. Inside the house, the baby was wailing at the top of her lungs. "All right, all right, all right, all right." Gloria had lost the fight.

Gloria is one of my oldest and closest friends and we had always been pretty honest with one another, but not, evidently, about the pain in our marriages. Gloria had never mentioned having problems with Ben. Things were always "great" whenever I called. When I asked her about Ben, she'd tell me, "He's such a help." "He's such a supportive man." Such a crock. Not that I hadn't handed her one too. I'd never disclosed to anyone the kind of tug of war my husband and I engaged in as we struggled with work and roles. Perhaps that was why I'd always felt so isolated and maladjusted, thinking that other dual-career couples were somehow sailing through the heady process of living together as equals while my husband and I struggled. Why were we pretending to have such perfect lives? Why were we afraid to tell each other what was really going on? What were we trying to hide?

It was, of course, easier to have insight into a fight that I heard as opposed to one that I fought. The heat of my own marital battles left me too drained to do anything but recover. I was too tired to analyze patterns and themes. Yet, the fundamental issue in Gloria and Ben's fight was so clear to me that I couldn't imagine why it had eluded me so often before. Gloria and Ben were fighting about power.

I had no framework in which to place my sudden insights; I just let the revelations fall where they might. I could identify the fact that both Gloria and I were professional women who were also trying to rear a child and be wives and homemakers. That was the crux of our domestic problems. I'd always believed the marital dissension I experienced stemmed from being stretched so far and not receiving the domestic cooperation from my husband that I needed. What was slowly dawning upon me as I listened to Gloria and Ben was that the opposition she was receiving from Ben was initiated because he resented her career success and felt threatened by it. Was that happening in my house too? "The job gets all of your attention," Ben had accused. You don't pay enough attention to me, is what he meant. Standing at Gloria's door, I realized both our husbands seemed to want the same things: a woman who was independent enough to work and traditional enough to be subservient in the home. "When I get what I want, maybe you'll get some help," Ben had said. He made it very clear. If Gloria gave him what he wanted, she'd be rewarded. And if she didn't . . .

He's mean, I thought. And he's in pain, I remembered. If his insecurity was responsible for some of the frustration his wife was experiencing, to what extent was Gloria contributing to her own problem? What was Gloria doing wrong, that he should feel so threatened? For that matter, what was I doing wrong? It would take me six years to answer that question. By that time I realized Gloria and I weren't alone and the stress we experienced is part of a national phenomenon that is decimating the marriages of newly emerging dual-career couples.

"Am I crazy?" Gloria asked me, handing me a cup of coffee and a piece of cake. A tall, slim woman with dark hair that framed her face in short, bouncy curls, she didn't even wait for an answer. I recognized the question as a rhetorical one that wives often ask each other.

"He expects me to do every fucking thing in this house," Gloria said, spitting out the words, reaching for the cigarettes she had quit smoking before the baby was born. "Last night, I had a late meeting at work, totally unexpected. I called Ben and asked him to pick up the baby from the sitter's, which started out being his job, except he passed it off to me because he was too busy. I had to listen to about fifteen minutes of his bitching on the phone about my always putting my job before my family and why can't I ever tell the boss no. Blah. Blah. Blah. Meanwhile, four nights out of five, Ben doesn't hit the door until after seven-thirty, okay? Well, he finally agrees to go get the baby. His child, right? When I do get home at eight-thirty, Ben and Bunnie are sprawled across the couch, sound asleep. This means she isn't going to sleep through the night and guess who is going to have to get up with her? She's soaking wet, hasn't been fed or bathed. And when I woke up Ben, do you know what he said? Do you know what the man said?"

" 'Hi, Honey,' " I replied in a mock manly voice, " 'dinner ready?' " Gloria shook her head, looked at me, and we both began to laugh.

We sat at the kitchen table for three hours, alternately laughing and crying, raging and whispering, rambling through our stories. We might have been reading from the same script, trying out for the same part of the beleaguered wife in some badly written melodrama. I had confided in one or two friends about my marriage before, but it was the first time I'd ever put my relationship under a microscope with another's and really examined what was there.

"Our marriage didn't start out like this. He's changed," said Gloria. "He went and got macho on me. In the beginning we did everything together. Cleaned house. Grocery shopped. Everything."

We analyzed why things had changed and when. "After I had the baby," Gloria declared, "it was as if everything that had gone on before, all the sharing was a lie. He saw me with the baby and began acting like, 'Aha! Gotcha now, kiddo!' " Gloria said. "Little by little, he has stopped doing almost everything around here." Gloria sighed. I nodded my agreement.

We discussed the subtleties of second-class domestic citizenship. "No matter how tired I am when I come home from work, when he wants to have sex, I'd better get up in that bedroom and perform. Now, when I want to have sex, that's a different matter." "Yes, yes," I said, nodding vigorously.

And we talked about working—about my job as an assistant editor for a corporate newspaper and hers as an attorney. We liked working. Gloria wanted to become a partner in her firm; I wanted to write bestselling novels. We had big,

big dreams and we were hell bent on seeing them come true. We acknowledged that we needed the cooperation of our husbands to make that happen and we were angry that they seemed to be reneging on their promises. "He's the one who used to think my being a lawyer was so great," said Gloria emphatically. "He used to help me study. Now he doesn't want to hear anything about the job. He gets angry if I talk about it.

"They want it both ways," Gloria remarked strongly, banging her hand down on the kitchen table. She got up and brought back two glasses and a bottle of wine. "Ben wants the money, so he wants me to work. He makes more than I do, but we need my salary to live the way we want to live. But even though I'm working, Ben expects the same kind of services that his father got from his wife. And my mother-in-law never worked outside of her house a day in her life.

"It's like he's afraid when he sees me winning," Gloria continued more quietly, sipping on the wine. "Three months ago, I got a really big case. He never congratulated me at all, just sort of grunted when I told him. Later in an argument, do you know what he said? 'Just because you're handling a big case now, you don't know everything.' Where do they come up with this stuff?"

In Gloria's kitchen, we women were blameless, above reproach. We were superwomen under siege. It was all their fault, the chauvinist pigs. Men just wanted to have their cake and eat it too. If we had broken promises to our husbands, we were not aware of it. If the men had a story to tell and

13

blame to dispense, we wouldn't own it. We knew only that they were afraid of our independence. They had better get their act together, we concluded darkly. Hell, we didn't have to take their nonsense. We earned our own money. We clinked glasses of Chablis: to not taking any more bullshit.

The whirring sound of the automated garage door signaled the time for my departure. Gloria walked me to the door. We were soulmates now, sisters in the struggle. She put her hand on my shoulder. "Do you ever feel like you're not going to make it?" she asked. "All the time," I answered. We stared at each other briefly, then she shrugged, whispering, "I'll talk with you soon," and closed the door.

A year later, Gloria's questions no longer seemed so rhetorical and my answer wasn't so pat. In 1979, enclosed spaces became the demons that terrorized my waking hours. I, who had never known a claustrophobic moment in my life, suddenly found myself incapacitated by the fear of being imprisoned and crushed by four walls. The terror had come out of nowhere. I was on the subway riding from my suburban Maryland home to work in downtown Washington, D.C., when it first happened. I looked into the faces of my fellow commuters wedged in beside me and felt a wave of uncontrollable panic overcome me like a sudden seizure that refused to be quelled. I was trapped in a speeding machine that was going to implode at any second.

The white man in the dark blue suit reading the *Washington Post* business section, the three young black girls giggling loudly at the end of the car, the arched-eyebrowed sophisticate with the bright red dragon-lady fingernails, all the people surrounding me would fall on top of me and cut off my breath. I would die slowly, painfully, unable to scream, gasping for air, trapped and overpowered. No air. No space. No escape. I was living my worst nightmare. Only by looking down at my feet, by forcing myself to recall bits of poetry and Bible verses, was I able to continue riding without screaming.

By the time I reached my stop, my clothes were clinging to my body and the pungent musk of my own fear was filling my nostrils. That panic would repeat itself again and again that year on other subways, buses, elevators, in traffic jams, and finally in crowds on the streets. I felt attacked by unseen forces. Stress, the softspoken psychiatric social worker told me. Slow down, she cautioned me.

Ha! Nineteen seventy-nine was a fast juggling act; some balls were in the air and some were hitting the floor. My marriage was four years old and failing. My fledgling career as a freelance writer was expanding, but my highly visible job was stressful. My three-year-old daughter was thriving. I was a mother, a wife, an employee, a moonlighter with big dreams. Outwardly, all the pieces of my life seemed to be in sync. I was the epitome of "You've come a long way, Baby." I was the feminist dream come to life. In reality, the balancing of the roles caused me more tension than I realized. Some of the balls were cracking as they hit the ground. And one of them was me.

The high ground and the low ground both tagged me that year. I applied for and won a National Endowment for the Arts literary grant. That award was the culmination of a year of No Doz nights and baggy-eyed dawns which saw me hunched over my typewriter, pumping out short stories. In addition, I had begun to sell articles to a few magazines. Since my days were filled with my job and early evening hours were filled with my daughter and husband, late at night was the only time I had for freelancing. The lack of sleep began to wear me down. I was wired from too much caffeine and guilt-laden from being too tired to enjoy my family. Still, when the letter came announcing that I'd won the grant, the long nights and short-tempered days were instantly forgotten. America had given me a green light. I was ecstatic.

But the cumulative toll of my all-night vigils wasn't so easily shrugged off. Less than two weeks later, I was fired from my job as assistant editor. My boss told me, in so many words, I didn't think like a manager, that I couldn't cut the mustard. Perhaps he was right. The protocol and office politics were a new world for me. I had been a classroom teacher previously. At the communications company, I was one of only three professional women on a staff of nearly twenty. I dressed for success with a vengeance, tried to do my homework and to at all times appear bright, aggressive, and responsible. I felt I had to be twice as good as the men to make it, but inwardly I wondered if I was even as good.

Perfectionist that I was, I had wanted to succeed in the

corporation. Being fired felt like a personal assault on my credentials and talents. Even the headiness of my newfound freedom and the exhilaration of earning a grant didn't mollify the damage to my self-esteem caused by being dismissed from my job. I had never been fired before. For several years the gloom of that failure hung over me like a shroud.

There was no space in my life for mourning or celebrating. I had a busybody of a three-year-old to take care of. I second-guessed my maternal abilities and agonized over whether I was being a good mother, the verdict still being out on whether good mothers were ever late picking up their toddlers from day care or skipped bathtime or neglected to read a bedtime story for two nights in a row. My child was moving past the baby stage and developing into a human being with her own awesome potential for success or failure. If I didn't do things absolutely right, she might catch a cold, have buck teeth, or not get into an Ivy League college. The responsibility weighed two tons and I couldn't shift the weight to anyone else. I was the mother. The mother. Was I doing it right? That's what I wanted to know.

I was clearly doing my career right. Magazine editors began calling me frequently and my typewriter clickety-clicked way into the night. I felt the pressure of having to steal time from my family in order to work. Gloria and I continued to compare notes and root for each other. Her career was booming too. She'd made all the correct political moves and was getting visibly closer to the partnership she sought. Yet, for reasons we couldn't understand, the more we won in our careers, the rockier our marriages became. Our stories still seemed to come from the same script. One month we put her life back together; the next mine, until finally the day came for both of us when there was nothing left to mend.

When my marriage ended in 1980 and Gloria's failed later that year it wasn't a coincidence, nor did I believe the forces that pulled our two families apart were particularly unique. In the years since that fateful day on Gloria's steps, I had begun to see the marriages of other dual-career couples I knew struggle, falter, then fall apart. It became clear to me that the dissolution of these marriages with their nearly identical plots and subplots is symptomatic of an urgent problem that is striking dual-career households with a startling degree of predictability.

All is not well with the two-career couple. In 1985, my work as a writer led me to explore the issue of the working couple for *Savvy* magazine. I interviewed thirty professional men and women, both married and divorced people, as well as psychologists and experts in the field of human relationships. The marriage counselors and therapists I spoke with agree that the added pressures these couples are facing threaten the stability of their families. These experts report they are seeing an increase in stress in working wives and that many of the husbands are suffering with diminished self-esteem. "It's a vicious cycle," said Audrey Chapman, a family therapist in Washington, D.C. "The women come in and begin by saying they feel tense, but ultimately they admit their marriages are in trouble because their husbands feel threatened by the independence their jobs create. Then the husbands come in and after you get them to talk, they say things like, 'All she cares about is work.' These guys feel neglected and they're angry." Many of the men I spoke with admitted that although they'd been committed to an equal relationship at the beginning of their marriages, they find it difficult to maintain their egalitarian stance, particularly when they feel their wives aren't giving them the kind of attention they want. The women I met declared they had carefully chosen men who promised to aid and support them in their professional ascendancy. They were angry because their husbands withdrew the support just when they needed it most. When they described the dynamics of their marriages, it becomes evident most don't have the kind of equality they thought they were promised.

Divorce is one concrete indicator of the level of dissatisfaction among married couples, although after 1½ decades, the national divorce rate has declined slightly, and stabilized in recent years according to the 1999 Rutgers National Marriage Project. In 1960, four years before the Civil Rights Act which outlawed racial and sexual discrimination in the workplace, 31.9 percent of all married women were in the labor force. In that year 42 women were divorced for every 1,000 marriages, according to the Census Bureau's report on marital status and living arrangements. In March 1997, 62.1 percent of married women with spouses present, 65.3 percent of married women with absent spouses, 66.8 percent of never-married women, and 74.5 percent of divorced women were in the labor force.[1]

In 1998, 8.2 percent of U.S. men were divorced as opposed to 10.3 percent women. The percentage of divorce is higher for females than for males primarily because divorced men are more likely to remarry than divorced women. Also, among those who do remarry, men generally do so sooner than women.[2]

Women accounted for 46.2 percent of total labor force participants in 1997 and are projected to comprise 48 percent by the year 2005.[3] For the first time in recent American history, more wives chose to work outside the home and many of these women are mothers. The Bureau of Labor Statistics says mothers with children under three are the fastest growing segment of the national workforce—46.8 percent of mothers with children under a year old are working outside the home.

Although one can anticipate that many women will take time out from their careers for childbearing and rearing, the trend in the past was for such absences to be relatively short, and the need for quality child care for working mothers ur-

---

[1] From Bureau of Labor Statistics, Employment and Earnings, various years.
[2] From Rutgers National Marriage Project & Bureau of the Census, Current Population Reports, Marital Status and Living Arrangements: March 1998 update.
[3] From Bureau of Labor Statistics, 1998.

gent. The trend for maternity leave has risen substantially since the enactment of the Family and Medical Leave Act (FMLA) in 1993; FMLA has helped an estimated twenty million Americans take time off from work to care for newborns, newly adopted children, and seriously ill family members, or to recover from their own illnesses, without losing their jobs or health insurance. But because the FMLA guarantees only unpaid leave (12 weeks), many women and men are still unable to take essential time off.[4]

Changes in the types of work help explain the rise of the female worker. Women held 76.3 percent of administrative jobs as of 1998. Women are four times as likely to hold administrative jobs as men.[5] However, in 1997, women held 10.6 percent of total board seats on Fortune 500 companies.[6] The ranks of professional women are also growing and many of the jobs women hold are white collar, since in 1998, college completion rates for women exceeded those for young men, 29 percent versus 25.6 percent respectively, for those aged 25–29.[7] Law schools and medical schools, once bastions of male exclusivity, report a huge increase in the number of female students. In 60 percent of married-couple families, both members are in the workforce.[8] Only 17 per-

---

[4] From National Partnership for Women and Families.
[5] From Bureau of Labor Statistics, 1998.
[6] Catalyst, 1997 Census of Women Board Directors of the Fortune 500.
[7] From Census Bureau, March 1998 update.
[8] From Catalyst (1997), 120 Wall Street, New York, New York 10005.

cent of all families conform to the 1950s model of a wage-earning dad, a stay-at-home mom, and one or more children.[9] As the percentage of female employees continues to rise, the question of the psychological implications of male displacement must be raised. Today's jobs are more demanding than ever for both sexes. Many workers experience . . . negative spillover from work. Twenty-eight percent often have not had the energy to do things with family or others; 36 percent of workers feel 'used up' at the end of the work-day.[10]

Moreover, women may witness a reversal of societal patterns. In February 1999, a jury awarded $375,000 to Kevin Knussman, a Maryland state trooper, who was refused extended leave to care for his newborn daughter because he was male.[11] There may be an ironic foreshadowing for American dual-career couples, that in an era when divorced men are increasingly dodging alimony and child support, working women may become saddled with payments of their own. The emotional impact on the masses of women who, claiming to want independence, are forced to go the full distance with it remains to be seen. Already dual-career couples are experiencing upheaval in their marriages as they struggle to make sense of relationships neither husbands nor wives find entirely comfortable.

---

[9] The Census Bureau, 1997.

[10] From Families and Work, "Ahead of the Curve."

[11] From Maryland Court Case Index (http://www.o12.net/stindex/stinx21.html).

It is clear the emergence of sizable numbers of career-minded wives has unsettled the balance of family power in America. Much has been written about the older, "traditional" male's resentment of his wife's entry into the labor force. That the Archie Bunkers of the world rail and lash out when their Ediths march off to the office has been so thoroughly depicted by the media it has become an established part of the American cultural landscape. Traditional men see the role of wife as one that must be homebound. These men are very clear: they don't want their wives to work and they are willing to foot the bill in order to keep them unemployed. What is shocking to younger women is the discovery that the "liberated" men they married—the men who once agreed to share in household chores, to delay having children to support their wives' ambitions, and to strive for egalitarian marriages—harbor many of the same resentments. The women I interviewed for my article had assiduously avoided pairing off with a traditional man. Some of them felt cheated when they ended up with Archie Bunker anyway. These women say they have encountered an insidious phenomenon which is straining their dual-career marriages—the husband who, in the initial stages of the relationship, appears to support and encourage his wife's professional development, only to turn on her when her career threatens his happiness. A friend in Boston termed the phenomenon succinctly: husband backlash.

The backlash results when husbands perceive a breach in the marital contract. Many act out when they feel they've lost control over their wives; for many that control defines their masculinity. That definition evolves from societal conditioning, the most easily identifiable component of backlash. Other factors contributing to the problem are corporate demands, lack of communication between marriage partners, and sexual role stereotypes. Backlash comes in escalating stages and takes many forms, but the most common include: belittling and sabotaging the wives' business efforts, manipulating wives into choosing between husbands' demands and their own professional goals; refusing to help with the household chores; withholding affection or making inconsiderate sexual demands; becoming emotionally and physically abusive; and having affairs with other women, particularly those perceived to be more submissive and traditional than their professional wives.

Some of the husbands I interviewed say they are justified in expressing dissatisfactions toward wives who have become professional automatons with misordered priorities. Most assert that they support the notion of equality for women, but at the same time they voice a common complaint: I didn't sign on to cheerlead a workaholic phantom who won't take my name, won't cook my meals, doesn't need my money, won't have my baby, and would rather make love to the job than to me.

Little is known about backlash, not only because it is a relatively new problem, but because husbands and wives, anxious to maintain the façade of a perfect marriage, deliberately attempt to hide it. Working women brag about how supportive their husbands are and husbands publically praise the achievements of their wives.

"My husband never tells people he has a problem with my success," said Margaret, 28, a sales manager for a high-tech firm in Denver. She had a forthright manner, a way of speaking her mind clearly and concisely. Her outspokenness was good for business, often not so good for her marriage. Her husband, David, 27, is in the same field and works for another company. Margaret says that in private, her husband acts out his resentment of her career in a number of ways, including downgrading her professional accomplishments and complaining he doesn't get enough sex and attention. "In all honesty, I don't talk about our problems with friends. I kind of gloss over them. I present Dave as a very supportive person, which he can be . . . at times. Everybody thinks we're the perfect couple."

There is something almost narcotizing about trying to portray the perfect couple while trying to escape the realities of married life. Margaret was like Gloria and me: trying to hide a keen sense of personal failure by pretending we didn't feel anything. What we felt was fear. Fear that our ineptitude would be discovered; fear that we didn't really deserve equality. Here we had all the ingredients the magazines said should make life exciting: husbands, children, wonderful jobs. And we still couldn't get it together. Perhaps we didn't deserve everything. Maybe we were afraid our husbands would try to impose tradition on us in worse ways than not washing the dishes. Just like our mothers and grandmothers, we took on the burden of failed marriages. Just like them, we opted to keep silent, to knuckle under. And because no one was saying, "No, you are not crazy. This is really happening," we felt isolated and powerless, as we struggled to understand what had gone wrong.

Not being able to talk about their feelings may explain why some women get caught up in the superwoman trap—attempting to keep the husband happy at home by fulfilling all the traditionally wifely roles, while working a job that demands equivalent or even greater attention. Repressed anger may also be the cause of explosive outbursts coming from husbands who can't hold in their feelings any longer. In addition, many husbands must balance their resentment against other factors: genuine pride in a wife's accomplishments, the advantages of a two-paycheck marriage, and a real belief in at least some of the tenets of feminism.

The issue of *Savvy* that carried my story, "Backlash in the Bedroom," had a provocative cover. A pretty young woman, slightly disheveled, a bit agitated around the eyes and mouth, was surrounded by a stack of law books, her glasses, a cup of coffee. The caption read: "It's 10 P.M. Do you know where your marriage is?" The issue sold out, the letters came from all over, and I appeared on *Oprah* to discuss the issue. Women knew what I was talking about; men knew what I was talking about. They all had stories to tell, questions they wanted answered. They all agreed: The cost of keeping backlash in the closet and ignoring its toll—failed marriages, impaired job performances, and increased stress for men, women, and children—is high. Too high. People want help.

I realized that if any solutions were to be forthcoming, I would have to find a larger group of men and women to interview and write a book about. With the promise of anonymity, more than 100 men and women agreed to discuss their lives and relationships and examine the issue of backlash in their marriages and, in some cases, former marriages.

The people I interviewed are, for the most part, big-city dwellers who, because of job opportunities, reside in metropolitan areas like Washington, D.C.; Atlanta; Boston; Philadelphia; New York; Los Angeles; Chicago; and Denver. The interviewees are mostly white, with a significant number of blacks participating and a few Asians and Hispanics. I visited the people in their homes, at their jobs, and in restaurants and talked for several hours in most cases. Sometimes I followed up interviews with telephone calls. Not all the women I interviewed had experienced backlash personally. Some had husbands who shared in household responsibilities and took genuine pride in their wives' accomplishments. More often than not, when I asked these wives what they believed had contributed to their husbands' egalitarian natures, most reported their husbands had always behaved the same way. They had no idea why their husbands were "liberated."

The internal struggles of dual-career couples echo women's quest for equality and economic parity with men in the larger society. Whether the price of female equality is the dissolution of their marriages is one of the crucial sociological questions of the decade. There is no map for the permanent transition of males from traditional to liberated. If the sixties and early seventies were an era of civil-rights gains for women, the eighties are the time when some men are reacting strongly to the feeling that their mates' gains are their losses. When men are feeling vulnerable, when they fear, irrationally or not, their mates are going to abandon them because of their own success, then they throw in the towel and revert to being what they best know how to be— traditional males. Not surprisingly, many women are caught off guard at the reversal. Because they thought women's hard-fought gains were permanent, they have no strategies, either collective or individual, for coping with husbands who fail to live up to their feminist expectations. Others, who always had the attitude that life in general and male behavior in particular holds no guarantees, may be able to handle their changed marital contracts with less stress.

LaVerne, 27, a young woman in Washington, D.C., had an easygoing, "give a little, get a little" attitude about male-female relationships and particularly her own marriage; she intrigued me because she seemed so effortlessly balanced. She had started her career in banking as a teller and was moving up quickly, upper management having taken notice of her efficient paperwork, and her irrepressible ebullience in dealing with customers. Her adeptness at blending different aspects of herself worked as well in her marriage as it did in business. Married nearly a year, she was six months pregnant and ecstatic about becoming a mother. She was more subdued about her husband's earnest attempts to be liberated. "Right now, he's in love and very happy," she said, her voice sending out the rhythms of the Caribbean nation where she was born. "He could eat me up with a spoon, that man. We go grocery shopping together, cook together, wash dishes and clothes together. Everything together. I praise him for everything, not that I think he's so great for washing dishes, but just to encourage him to keep on. I hope this lasts forever, but listen, men from my country are macho, my dear. He may change. If he does, okay," LaVerne said with a smart clap of her hands, "I'll do the housekeeping. But," she added, "he'll have to do something else."

LaVerne had spent her youth and adolescence in a land with a sunnier clime and slower pace, where even today, traditional sex roles remain virtually unchallenged. Perhaps that can explain why her attitude is more fluid than fixed. LaVerne came to America just in time to reap the benefits of the women's movement without having had to participate in it. If American women are outraged that male support of their equality is wavering, it is perhaps because they lived through the early days of the women's movement. For many, the sixties and seventies represent a period when they made a tremendous emotional investment in shaping their own futures. The payoff they expected still eludes them.

2

How We Got Here: From Women's Lib to Backlash

Raina's New York apartment was a tribute to commitment, from the symbolic art and posters on her walls to the mix of politically righteous titles spilling out of her bookshelves onto the small coffee table and even the floor. The books shouted for an end to apartheid, demanded a nuclear freeze, and cried for food to feed the starving in Africa. Every inch of space in the apartment declared that the occupants stood for something.

Unlike LaVerne, the West Indian banker, Raina had been an active participant in the women's movement. As we sat sipping tea in the living room while her husband cooked in the kitchen, she told me that feminism had not only shaped her life, it had defined her. And she had stumbled upon it quite unexpectedly: "For my eighth-grade graduation, one of my mother's friends gave me a copy of *Sisterhood Is Powerful*. I spent the summer reading the book and all the way through I kept having the famous feminist click of recognition. The book gave a name to things I'd been feeling all of my life."

Perhaps more than anything else, the concepts of the women's movement presented Raina with an alternative to the kind of oppression her mother had been forced to accept. "My parents had always been the role model for what I *didn't* want. Their marriage was awful. My mother had to account for everything in her life. My father had complete control over her behavior. He wanted her at home, so she never got to go anywhere. She had to do everything in the house: cook, clean, wash, take care of the kids. Everything. He never helped her. My father didn't want my mother to have friends. She met the woman who gave me the book during one of her many attempts to get her eighth-grade diploma. My father had nagged and beaten her up until she stopped going to school. That's how he stopped her from doing anything he didn't want her to do."

Robin Morgan's book clarified the issues that had puzzled, rankled, and angered Raina for years: the unfairness she'd always seen and felt, but had never spoken out about; the way the boys got away with not doing dishes; the way her father beat her mother; why she couldn't become a scientist.

"I was an atypical little girl. I wasn't into dolls. There was this science guy on television at the time, Mr. Wizard. He'd pour stuff into beakers and they would start smoking and bubbling. I remember being little and watching Mr. Wizard and thinking, 'I want to do that. Take the dolls back. Give me some beakers.' "

But the world of the fifties wasn't geared for female scientists. Though she wanted more, as a child Raina couldn't fight the steady steering toward conventional femininity, the ribbons and ruffles, the curtsies and dolls. Like Raina, millions of young girls learned—and still learn—that they have a duty to make themselves physically and emotionally appealing to men. From the time mothers admonish their daughters not to be "tomboys," to let the boys beat them at checkers, to endure the pain of sleeping on rollers or straightening kinky hair, girls learn society's message to them: be submissive, beautiful, and ladylike if you want boys to like you.

"In junior high, around 1957, I put together a group called 'The Career Club,' " recalled Amy, 43. "It was very apparent that careers for women were limited. When we'd try to get businesses to let us come in and talk with their managers, we were told there were no women in the field, so we shouldn't bother. The club wasn't popular. Only eight girls out of a class of four hundred were members. Students nicknamed it 'The Queers Club.' That was the first time I ever heard that label, homosexuality, when women try to take themselves seriously."

Research shows that girls expect to do less well at a variety of tasks than boys . . . women tend to underestimate their [abilities], and more often internalize failure and write off success.[12] They are encouraged to negate the more aggressive sides of their personalities: their ambition, drive, and anger. The reward for a young girl's being malleable and needy is that a man will find her attractive enough to protect and to prolong her childlike status. The alternative—being alone—is a powerful deterrent to female independence. "The message I got growing up was that it was preferable for a woman to be married," said Amy. "If you were too smart or cocky, you'd threaten off any potential suitors. I got this message from my mother, aunts, my friends' parents. When I showed an interest in the law, my girlfriend's father, who was an attorney, said, 'Oh, no, you mustn't be an attorney. It's too hard and competitive.' "

The majority of women are molded for dependency, but it is important to note that some are not. Some black women, for example, are trained by both their mothers and fathers to be independent, ambitious, and under no circumstances believe that a man will take care of them. Because racism often limits black men's economic opportunities even more than black women's, young girls are taught they have to take care of themselves, whether they marry or not. The relationships of black women have often suffered because of the difficult balancing they must do. In the March 1982 issue of *Essence*, authors Lenore Jenkins-Abramson and Elaine Ray

---

[12] From *She Works, He Works* (Barnett, 1998).

wrote in their article, "When Your Career Collides with Your Man's Ego,"

> Traditionally, black women have been workers and homemakers, a dual role that has imposed tremendous burdens on some of us. But this dual role has often been a bone of contention between us and our men. Some of us have been criticized for devoting too much time and energy to our work and not enough time to our mates or families. As a result of us having to balance our careers and romantic lives, we have become well equipped to handle the demands of both. But our relationships with our mates have frequently suffered from severe unresolved conflicts.
>
> At the root of these conflicts is the fact that despite women's changing roles—many of our men still have traditional attitudes about where our work/home priorities should lie. Many agree that we should work—just as our mothers did—but that our aspirations should not exceed our mates' or infringe on our duties as housekeepers and mothers.

Perhaps in an effort to escape the marital conflicts that have slowly begun to engulf the total society, black women, too, fantasized about being swept off their feet and taken care of by a man. The dream of an all-powerful Prince Charming is so culturally persuasive, so insistent, so supported by media images as well as cultural mythology, that no group escapes being swayed by it.

The women's movement clarified for Raina, who is black,

that the force keeping her pinned to a tiny spot was orga-
nized, systematized, and attacked all women in the same
way. The force had a name: oppression. More important,
there was a way to fight it. "By the time I got back to school
in September I was a changed person," she said. "I was rad-
icalized. I cut my hair very, very short and I became this
raving feminist maniac. There was a period in my life where
everyone in school thought I was a lesbian and I half thought
it myself, until I realized I wasn't attracted to women." She
was attracted to power. "I became the head of every student
project in my school and started a women's group to raise
consciousness. I was going to change the world."

Her father, a hostile man who did odd jobs and who
Raina suspected drank secretly and steadily, was both mys-
tified and appalled. He looked at his daughter's closely
cropped hair with its defiant curls, her jeans and boots, her
unpainted face, the grim line of her mouth. " 'What's wrong
with you, girl?' " Raina said, holding her teacup in her lap,
mimicking her father's gruffness and grimace, his fear. She
let the words, so weighted with a history that was both ex-
cruciatingly personal and yet sublimely universal, hang in the
air above the plate of cookies she'd placed in front of us.

Raina and her father battled for months over her mannish-
looking hair and clothes, her outrageous statements and blatant disrespect. The walls of the small, crowded apartment
shook with his loud, bellowing outrage and Raina's equally
loud defiance. For her father to admit—even to himself—
that he couldn't control any female was difficult for him to

accept. His daughter's intransigence was humiliating and frustrating. Hard headed, that's what she was, he thundered. He threw up his hands in disgust, but not before he'd given Raina what he thought was a final, chilling prediction. "One night after we'd had another one of our big blowups and my newly acquired feminist logic had left him totally bewildered and utterly exasperated, he yelled, 'You're crazy! No man in his right mind is ever going to marry you!' " Facing her father's contorted face, she heard another click. When she answered him, Raina felt light-headed and utterly free. "I looked him dead in his eyes and said, 'Fine.' "

What was propelling Raina beyond the boundaries of her father's values to the place where his rage and shaking fists couldn't touch her was her discovery of her own female power, her tremulous decision to define herself. As I listened to Raina, I realized I had lived her feelings, if not her story. The texture of her words took me back to the space inside myself where I could feel the sixties and seventies, the memories of that era's activism and my own tentative stumbling toward a new kind of womanhood. I could hear Hendrix and Baez, smell burning incense and the biting odor of grass wafting through campus dorms. I could see brass medallions, fashioned in the symbol of peace, and furiously colored dashikis, mile-high afros, wildly waving fists. And I saw women with soft, unfettered breasts underneath tie-dyed cotton shirts, talking quietly in support groups, mouthing the strange-sounding new title of Ms., screaming and yelling and raising their fists. If Raina's transformation had come suddenly, others had quieter cues and their baptism in feminism was more gradual.

"There wasn't just one event," recalled Leonora, a psychologist. "I slowly had a general consciousness-raising based on reading articles and discussions with other women. There was a group of three or four women who all had relationships with men. I remember us being very supportive of each other and laughing and crying together over our struggle. We came to have similar views about negotiating with men."

The second phase of the women's movement picked up where feminists had left off in the earlier part of the century. Early radical feminists blazed a political path and shaped an agenda that gradually was embraced by more moderate women. Even traditional women who eschewed feminism were changed by its powerful concepts. On college campuses across the nation young women sat in the women's studies courses they'd demanded, learning more about themselves and their status, and the women's movement won more and more converts.

Not all women embraced feminism easily. Many had difficulty recognizing and identifying with their own subservience. "I came from a very isolated, white upper-middle-class community," said Greta, 41. "When I went to work for a large corporation they sent me to train in Newark. It was the first time I'd ever been around bright black people or Jews. That was the most wonderful experience. Around that time, the mid-sixties, I was beginning to get concepts from the women's movement but I had a hard time with it. I acted out my liberal side with the race issue. At work, I was playing the little-girl role. I would go to the grocery store and buy the coffee for the staff meeting. I would pick people up at the airport. I had a hard time identifying this subservient role as a woman's issue."

Many women received forceful opposition from the men in their lives when they began to react to feminism. "I first began to be interested in the women's movement in 1973, after my husband and I were separated," Amy recalled. "I was pregnant with my second child and I went to take Lamaze classes by myself. It was traumatic being around all the couples. I went back, though, and I found another woman who was there alone. The result was that she and I became partners. I took her to the hospital and coached her and she did the same for me.

"Our friendship continued after I got back with my husband. She got involved in the feminist movement and began to talk to me about it. That threatened my husband fiercely. One time when I was leaving to have dinner with her and a friend he said, 'Go ahead and be a dyke if you want to.' "

The suffragettes of the early twentieth century had identified lack of voting power for women as the cause of their oppression, and the male politicians who sought to prevent women from voting as the enemy. The feminists of the sixties had new demands and new opponents. They wanted equal access to education, jobs, and political office. They wanted the passage of the equal rights amendment. The Civil Rights Bill of 1964, which promised access to educational and employment opportunities for all, regardless of race or sex, gave them powerful support. It was the impetus for affirmative-action guidelines that granted women and minorities the chance to catch up with white males in the society.

Women also began to realize that there was inequality in every facet of their lives. Away from politics and university classrooms and corporate offices, the struggle for women's equality began to heat up in the far more intimate sphere of personal relationships. Through support groups and consciousness-raising sessions, women bonded to each other and created an unprecedented feeling of sisterhood. Their closeness wasn't extended to men; in fact, it was characterized by a blatant "them against us" mentality. At the same time women were strengthening their own friendships, they were declaring men the enemy, specifically the males in their own homes—their fathers, brothers, lovers, and husbands. It was these "male chauvinist pigs" who perpetuated their economic and emotional subserviency. While women admitted some of their own weaknesses, most feminists in the early days of the movement held men responsible for their second-class condition. Many of them were able to feel their rage and express it for the first time. "I got really mad from the women's movement," Ann, a clinical social worker, remarked. "I learned that the exchange wasn't equal; women were getting ripped off. I did a lot of screaming and ranting at men during that time."

Admittedly, this angry period was short-lived, but it set a tone that lingered long after the anger had dissipated. "The women's movement didn't change my ideas per se, but it opened up avenues for me," said Ruth, the manager of a radio station. "It absolutely changed my feelings about my mom's lot. There was no way I was ever going to do everything in the house." As employment opportunity increased, more and more women began to see themselves in nontraditional careers. For that kind of aspirations to lead anywhere, they needed to share their lives with a new kind of man and leave behind the inequities of traditional relationships. Leonora said, "The women's movement changed me. I began to realize it was crazy for anyone to assume I would take care of all the housework and childcare. Even though I'd grown up in a traditional home, I began to feel there should be some compromise and negotiating around those issues."

The macho man who stoically shouldered the burden of protecting his children while his wife took care of the home and reared their children wasn't what was wanted. In midnight dorm sessions, afternoon coffee klatches, and lunchhour kibbitzes, women began to pinpoint some of the changes that were necessary to accommodate their new development. Feminists declared that if they were going to be able to compete in the workplace, men had to participate equally in housework and childcare. And they attacked many of the traditions that seemed symbolic of their oppression, including the use of Miss and Mrs., the taking of male surnames after marriage, and wedding rituals like "giving the bride away." "The night before my wedding I read the ceremony and I didn't like what I was agreeing to do," said Monica, now 41. "I told the minister I was going to rewrite my vows. I wasn't going to say the word *obey*."

Some women had trouble with such rebelliousness. Others didn't know how to proceed to get what they wanted. The climate, however, changed radically. Women moved forward propelled by their ideas and a continuing rage that would later boomerang in their faces.

To be sure, there were men who didn't have to be confronted, because they reacted to feminism so positively. "The women's movement first hit me when I was an undergraduate, back in 1968," said Dr. Harry W. Brod, at the time assistant professor of the Study of Women and Men in Society at the University of Southern California. "Seeing the sisterhood that was prevalent among women, I realized men didn't have those kind of close relationships. The women's movement sensitized me to the negative aspects of male socialization—the competitiveness, aggressiveness, and violence."

Across the country during the late sixties and seventies, men clustered in church basements and counseling centers to discuss their relationships with their wives and children and talk about what it felt like to be men. For the first time some college-educated men began to choose not to go into the corporate fast lane and began to express a desire to develop themselves beyond the role of competitive, achieving entities. More divorced fathers asked for custody of their children in the seventies than ever before, and not just to avoid paying child support. Many didn't want to be cheated out of the joys of fatherhood.

Brod's discovery of feminism led him to join with a few

men who saw the women's movement as the impetus for their own emotional liberation. As a member of the National Organization of Changing Men, a group that functioned from approximately 1975 to 1985, Brod helped promote new concepts of maleness that included being nurturing, supportive of feminist goals, and against male violence.[13] Brod was convinced that feminism and the changing status of women had been beneficial for men, but he realized that not all men agreed with him and admitted the membership of NOCM was less than a thousand and that many of the members were gay. "The majority of men reacted to the women's movement and women's new demands by feeling threatened. They supported equal pay for equal work, but women entering the workforce frightened them. Being the breadwinner is a strong part of the core of male identity." And, one might add, manliness is still measured by achievement in the workplace.

From the time mothers and fathers admonish their sons not to cry and to act like a man, boys learn society's lesson: do not display emotion, be aggressive, be powerful if you want to be a man. To be otherwise relegates boys to the ranks of sissies—a shameful fate to be avoided at all costs. While men feel the same range of emotions as women, they

---

[13] Info on NOCM taken from Michigan State University Libraries, Special Collections Division, The Changing Men Collection of research materials, 100 Library, East Lansing, MI 48824.

learn early on that they must internalize most of them. Anger is the one reaction that has been certified acceptable for males to feel and express. What isn't all right is for men to display fear or vulnerability.

As little girls are trained to be submissive in their relationships with men, so boys are taught that manhood requires that they control women. So strong is the message that some men cannot feel manly unless women are dependent upon them.

Rejecting stereotypes of dependence and subservience for themselves, many women had to convince prospective mates to agree to an equal relationship. "I grew up in a male-dominated household, seeing my mother acquiesce and be subservient," recalled Roger, a chiropractor. "Although I was a child of the liberated sixties and seventies, I still had a problem dealing with strong, aggressive women. I was intimidated by them."

"Back in the seventies when Cecilia and I first moved in together we had our first big argument," said Willis, 36, a medical researcher. "She told me I had to clean up after myself. That was a big shock. I think subliminally I probably expected my lover or wife would do this for me."

"I knew Willis when he lived in a platonic roommate situation with my sister and another male," explained Cecilia. "My sister had taken on the mother role. Willis has a tendency to be very cavalier about leaving things around. My sister was Miss Tidy Tidy. She cleaned up after him. When we moved in together and he started leaving his things all over the place and, in general, not helping out with the housework, I hit the ceiling. I made it clear that under no circumstances would I clean up after him."

Some women conveyed their need for a different kind of mate with straightforward logic. Others coerced and manipulated their way to pseudoequality in their relationships. And many women pushed for a more egalitarian relationship with angry demands. They issued ultimatums to hapless suitors: no equality, no romance.

Cecilia, like a lot of young women whose courtships took place in the sixties and seventies, made equality an issue in her relationship. Willis agreed to cooperate with her because he wanted to be with her, but also because sharing the household chores appealed to his sense of fair play. Willis had been reared with many of the same traditional values as his father but he was more open to the feminist message partly because it was "in the air," as it had not been in his father's time. The other factor may have been that baby boomers, particularly those who attended college, were more open to including the egalitarian relationship. This was the first generation of men to massively resist going to war, to be somewhat sensitized by a civil-rights movement that pointed a finger squarely at white male oppression and racism, to call for the legalization of marijuana, and, for some, to declare themselves gay and proud. Older men shook their heads in disbelief. What was happening? they wondered. But in the liberal political atmosphere of the country, it became more acceptable for women and men alike to espouse a philosophy of equality for all people, including women. The times had as much to do with men's liberated behavior in the sixties and seventies as did the women in their lives. When women cried out for fair play from their lovers, many men were persuaded to act and talk as if they were liberated.

It seemed that the age of the egalitarian couple had arrived. As politicized women accepted wooing, it was clear that the ritual of romance had changed. The emerging "equal" career-minded young woman of the sixties and seventies, often only recently removed from campus activism, didn't just want to hear about how beautiful her eyes were. What she was more interested in hearing was how much freedom there would be in any prospective marriage. A lot of men went along with their fervently independent girlfriends. They sighed somewhat uncomfortably and stopped opening car doors; they let these new women pick up the tabs at restaurants and even felt guilty about the sins of their fathers.

It was a heady time of turned tables and scintillating male-female repartee. As feminist women and liberated men became engaged, a new marital contract emerged. This one called for the sharing of housework and childcare; dual freedom to achieve professionally; the option for a woman to delay childbirth so that she might further her career. The demands and requests for change were almost entirely hers because, after all, women were the ones who'd been oppressed.

But the men who were agreeing to these conditions had

not figured out what they would get out of the deal—or what they'd lose. Courtship is supposed to be a time to test what marriage will be like. As it turned out, there was no way for these couples to foresee the real future of their egalitarian relationships. "My husband and I met at my aunt's house in the seventies," said Brenda, 37. "At the time, I had my Ph.D. and was teaching at a university. He had an administrative position with a university and had his master's degree. We had a wholesome relationship. We took each other's work into consideration. He had no problem with the fact that I was called doctor. He understood I didn't like housework and agreed that we'd share. He understood I didn't want any kids and that my career was very important to me. Everything went well—for about a year."

Some egalitarian marriages seem to have stuck with the feminist contract and to have remained intact for many years. "A lot of couples have felt their way along. Husbands and wives have stayed communicative enough to monitor their own growth," says Michael Hughes, a psychotherapist and family counselor from Los Angeles who treats many males with identity problems. After marriage, egalitarian ideals began unraveling, pulled apart by a number of factors. The expectation that it would be easy to sustain this new kind of marriage was its undoing. "The husbands and wives in these unions were baby boomers—a group with a distinct cultural and socioeconomic orientation," explains Hughes. "We all grew up watching television, having things hawked at us. We were raised to be consumers—to instantly buy whatever we wanted. A lot of baby boomers subscribed to the notion that they could have everything easily. With the dual-career marriage, they got frustrated because it wasn't easy. As opposed to following knowingly and agreeably in the footsteps of their parents and other adult models, couples of the seventies found themselves confronted with the shock that they had to continue to draw a map as they went along. They were in uncharted waters."

No one had yet figured out exactly what liberated husbands and wives required of each other. Slowly couples began to see the magnitude of the change in life-style they were attempting. It was one thing for a girlfriend to pay for an occasional date, quite another for a wife to reject her husband's name forever. Women who grew up expecting to be financially provided for by their husbands were subliminally anxious at the prospect of working for the rest of their lives. Men and women had been reared to live their lives under far different circumstances and with different kinds of people. The brave new world was scary. In homes across the nation, couples were reeling as they hit the stumbling blocks in their paths.

Then, the political landscape began to change and as liberalism faded from the national scene, opposition to women's equality increased. The end of the Kennedy/Johnson years ushered in an era of challenges to affirmative action and an antifeminist zeal. Fundamentalists vigorously and violently attacked legalized abortions. The White House opposed ERA and a new image of the genteel and ultrafeminine woman seemed to find favor in some circles. Though many of them would deny it, that picture of traditional feminity was to become more appealing to many men in egalitarian relationships. As the seventies drew to a close, the novelty of doing the dishes was wearing off and the drudgery setting in. Men began to feel more and more uncomfortable with their marriages and their liberated wives.

Women realized their husbands' commitment to egalitarianism was faltering. They also had many conflicts about their own roles and some women were finding it hard to leave room for their husbands around the edges of their commitment to their careers. As both partners failed to live up to the other's expectations and fantasies, they felt shortchanged. The pull of the times, the clashing of new and old value systems began eroding the tenuous bargain men and women had attempted to strike. The changes men and women were going through were leading them in opposite directions.

3

The Job or the Marriage,
Which Is More Impo[rtant?]

It was the kind of clear, languid Indian su[mmer] that makes living through the sweltering[...] Washington August worthwhile. I wa[s...] front steps, but my mind was not on the [...] stead, I alternated between looking at my [...] ning the street for the mailman who [...] particular day, be carrying my life in his ba[...]

At last I saw him, mail pouch over his s[...] with my neighbor for what seemed an eter[...] shout, "Hurry up!" down the long, tree-li[ned...] he finally arrived at my door, I grabbed th[...] he gave me, nodded quickly, and ducked ins[...] tically searched until finally I found what I [...]

On the cover of the magazine I held in my hand a pretty

woman smiled at me. I smiled back. Opening the magazine, I ran my fingers down the table of contents, flipping through pages until I found what I'd been dreaming about for five years. There it was. My name. My story. I had survived five years of rejection slips with no assurance that I'd ever be published. And now, finally, my persistence was paying off. Tingling with excitement, I hugged the magazine to me as I dialed my husband's work number. He'd helped me through all the bad times. I wanted him to be the first to share my good news.

"You're good," my husband would tell me, when yet another rejection would come in the mail. He would patiently listen whenever I wanted to read a short story aloud. His advice, whether to change a word, drop a sentence, or move a paragraph around, was always thoughtful and concerned. His reassurance revived my hope when I felt it slipping away. Naturally, I did the same for him, listening and encouraging as he described his dreams and aspirations. I ran his errands, typed his projects, and brought home from the library the books he needed. Although we were in separate fields, we were a team; our destiny was to make our dreams come true together.

My own career seemed launched. A year after my first article was published, I was writing for several publications and the editors of a prominent women's magazine had summoned me to New York where, over elegant meals, we discussed my story ideas. It was heady stuff for a young woman with a young marriage.

As my writing began to take more and more of my time, however, I had less time to root for anybody's dream but my own. Our baby was born in November. While she slept or cooed in her playpen, my husband and I knocked down the walls, stripped the woodwork, sanded the floors, and stained the woodwork of the "fixer" house we'd bought. The din and bustle of the reconstruction blocked out a lot of what was happening between us. If our tempers flared more than usual, if we had become more distant and emotionally unavailable to each other during this period of banging and hammering and knocking out walls, well, it was really too noisy and inconvenient to tell. It was only later, months later, when our yuppie castle was silent and clean and pretty that the harshness in our voices really became noticeable. It occurred to me then that something was going wrong, but I didn't know what. It was far more pleasant to stare out the new picture window than contemplate nagging problems. On the newly added sun porch, I read and reread my latest submission; I was so engrossed in my work I failed to recognize that my own marriage, like marriages across the country, was under severe pressure. My metamorphosis into a successful writer was changing me, as it was changing many liberated women, from an idealist to a harried professional. At the same time this was happening, the commitment of liberated men was being eroded. In my case, it was hastened by one half of the dream coming true—my half.

It was the dual-career couple's immersion in the workforce that made clear the enormous adjustments that would have to be made in the traditional concept of marriage. As women clamored to take advantage of the job opportunities that came their way, many of them, even feminists, were stunned by the demands of their jobs. Some women panicked when they realized what working men and women knew all the time—that work demands an enormous amount of time and energy. Young women turned to their mates for support and encouragement, but their husbands were no less hampered by a time-and-energy crunch. The difference was that the men had been socialized to expect that a job would demand a great deal from them. What further stunned many liberated wives was to discover that their husbands responded to stress overload as their fathers had: by coming home late and collapsing across a couch with the television on, waiting for dinner to be served. In turn, males experienced a severe shock when their wives did not devote themselves totally to their needs, as their mothers had done for their fathers. While husbands lay on that couch, not only was there no one to bring them a beer, but in many cases their exhausted wives were stretched out beside them.

Bonnie said that several years ago she and her husband were "living on a tightrope" because of the demands of their careers. She had just become the manager of a crew of radio technicians and her husband was a photographer. All day long they moved in their separate spheres, each totally immersed in the work. By nightfall, she said they were so drained they could offer each other little companionship. "Both of us were saying to each other, 'Why don't you bring a little of that work energy into the house?' We were more married to the jobs than we were to each other. The work, with its stress and exhaustion, was leaning on our sexual identity. We lost track of Bonnie and Paul. We became professionals who just happened to be living together. Lots of times we've been close to saying, 'I can't take it anymore.' Not each other but the stress."

Stunned by these schedules, some idealistic, first-time professionals declared they would short-circuit their own ambitions to preserve "quality" in their lives and maintain their fifty-fifty marriages. Most soon discovered that their decision to limit their ambition didn't preclude a job's imposing a grueling schedule on them. For many people, the laid-back life-style was shortlived as economics forced husbands and wives to compete harder. Baby boomers became enmeshed in corporations and they found themselves trapped in a work life that included the late hours, travel, and after-hours socializing that is standard in most companies. Home life was often a boring routine with husbands and wives in a state of near collapse and neither receiving the nurturance they needed. Couples were forced to direct their energies toward constant preparation for the next day's work rather than toward each other. It is not that these "realities" of life were new—people who work come home tired at night; and it's hard to sustain a romance in the workaday world. The problem has a new edge for modern families because the *expectations* were different, because the ideal life that educated middle-class men and women envisioned included shared careers—but not daily drudgery. Women believed that the two-career marriage would be able to handle diapers and dirty dishes more gracefully than had ever been done before because those chores would be shared. Men secretly believed they'd be exempt from those duties. Many had fantasized so much about their careers that they'd never imagined the life they'd lead away from work.

"A typical day between September and June, we get up at six-thirty," said Linda, a psychological counselor. "My husband goes downstairs and makes coffee and fixes our little girl's lunch. Then I wake up our daughter. I get dressed and help her get dressed. We all end up upstairs in our bedroom between seven and seven-thirty. We're back downstairs between seven-thirty and eight to get breakfast. Three days a week he takes her to school. The other two days I take her. One of us picks her up, depending on who's working later. Two nights a week, I work late and don't get in until around eight. Those are the days when both of us are really beat, me because I worked longer and him because he's been alone with an energetic five-year-old. Ninety percent of the time, I fix dinner; ten percent of the time he brings something in. We try to get our daughter in bed by eight-thirty. Then if we're not totally exhausted, and most nights we are, we'll have another glass of wine and fall asleep in front of the television."

Young couples making the transition from courtship to married life have always had difficulty setting aside time for their relationship. When both people work, they seem resigned to not being able to make emotional contact. "We don't have time to really talk," said one man with a shrug. "We haven't taken a vacation together since we got married." Men who expected their wives to focus attention on *their* careers were frustrated when they only attended to their own. As the daily grind began to wear couples down, they felt attacked by each other and outsiders.

Professional stress is the common experience of most working wives. Like men they fight deadlines and office politics, but unlike their husbands, they face something far more debilitating. They say that as newcomers to the corporate arena they must survive in a hostile, sexist work environment that demands they be twice as good as men just to stay even and a lot more if they are to ascend in their companies. Most women in corporations and professions speak of having to constantly prove themselves at their jobs. These women declare that the system hasn't changed to accommodate them. They must go after success on traditional male terms without the mainstay support that has afforded older men their achievements: a stay-at-home wife who augments her husband's professional life by dedicating herself to his needs. Their husbands must contend with these same handicaps and they, too, feel cheated. Yet conformity is even more difficult for women. Corporations don't take into consideration that the professional is a wife, perhaps a mother with traditional demands on her time and energy. Female professionals must compete with males who often resent their presence and must report to bosses who don't have empathy for their struggle.

Many working wives say they are experiencing varying degrees of gender shock, isolation, and alienation as they attempt to acclimate themselves professionally and assimilate into organizations that reward uniformity—white male uniformity. Although feminists demanded it, few people really expected women would become insiders in the corporation and fewer still understood what overcoming the barriers of discrimination would mean for them. It may have appeared that women glided easily from domesticity and subservience to the world of earning their own way and being in charge, but the transition has been far from smooth. Women professionals say the same sexism that kept them out of corporations for years is still very much alive.

"The majority of the department heads at my station are white males," said a black television producer for a major network station. "They look at women differently, maybe even more than they discriminate because of race. They don't have as much appreciation for the abilities of women. If I have to make a presentation, I'm drilled unnecessarily. When I needed a new camera, I had to make a thorough presentation as to why I needed it to a committee of men and when I did, these guys proceeded to throw highly technical and mostly unnecessary questions at me. It was ludicrous. Meanwhile, the male news director made a far less thorough presentation for his camera and it was immediately accepted. I definitely feel that if I'd been a white male, by now I'd be a station manager. I've been in the industry for nearly twenty-two years. I'm smart. By this time I should be a station manager or qualified as one. I haven't even reached the step below that job."

A newspaper reporter from New York said, "Certain types of reporting are relegated to women. You're not given an assignment because it's deemed too important to go to a woman."

An article in the *New York Times* described the subtle discrimination that female physicians encountered at school and work. They declared that while many of their male colleagues are accepting of them, a significant number try to impede their progress, causing them additional strain in a stressful profession. Female executives cite the following top three factors still holding women back: male stereotyping and preconceptions of women (52 percent); exclusion from informal networks of communications (49 percent); and lack of significant general management/line experience (47 percent).[14]

As white women moved away from the security of the domestic lives they were reared for and some black women began to surpass the accomplishments of black men, they became isolated in their old world. Many female professionals, particularly those in upper-middle and upper management, have few people to confide in. Their parents, especially their mothers who've always been full-time homemakers, don't understand the kind of problems they are having.

---

[14] From 1996 Catalyst study.

Many suffer from a lack of self-esteem. One older doctor who was interviewed for the *New York Times* article said succinctly, "Women physicians are never more competent than they are confident."

As they move up the corporate ladder, women also become distant from other women who work in lower positions in the same company. "I've felt isolated as a woman," said Kelly, 34, a manager for an automotive company. "I remember when I went to work for the company I'm with and I was the only woman in the department. I felt that all the men were watching and assessing me. I couldn't confide in anyone. The guys I managed were sitting there waiting for me to fall on my face. My peers wouldn't help me. They resented me because I was young, female, and a manager destined to be an executive in the organization when they knew they'd peaked out. Here I was new in the city and the job, and so lonely I could have died. At night, I used to call my girlfriends back home and cry on the telephone." One strategy to overcome racism and sexism is for women networking and mentoring each other. Although a male executive occasionally will mentor a female employee, statistics overwhelmingly support the notion that it is largely women who are willing to enter into a safe, nurturing work relationship of showing another woman employee the ropes and how things "really work."[15]

---

[15] From Advancing Women, International Business and Career Community News, Networking & Strategy For Women, (210) 822-1103 (t); (210) 821-5119 (f).

The isolation is understandable. In many blue-collar jobs as well as professions, women are sparsely represented. The higher one climbs in a corporation, the fewer women there are. Typical is the case of medical school facilities. Even though the percentage of female medical students had more than doubled from 1969 to 1979, the percentage of full-time female faculty members in medical schools had only risen from about 12 percent to 17 percent.

Men who feel and maintain a commitment to their wives and children are just as isolated. Although a majority of men (56 percent) reported that having a working wife had a positive impact on their careers,[16] in the competitive work environment of the American corporation, men are expected to sacrifice their personal lives to advance their careers. If they seem unwilling to do so, if they want to leave early to pick up their children or are reluctant to work weekends because they want to spend time with their wives, they are immediately suspect. Bosses and co-workers aren't likely to be sympathetic and their male friends may not understand either. Forty-one million employees in the private workforce (almost 43 percent) are not protected by the Family and Medical Leave Act.[17] Men may particularly resent female co-workers who push for an easier load just because they are women.

---

[16] From Catalyst (Bureau of Labor Statistics 1997).
[17] From Equal Rights Advocates.

Though women do find support from other working women, some people, particularly if they are homemakers, are far from helpful. "I've noticed that a lot of girlfriends who started their careers when I did have dropped out to have babies," said Jennifer, the manager in a computer firm in Los Angeles. "When I talk with them about my problems on the job or in my marriage they can't relate. Sometimes they're far from sympathetic. It's like they're waiting for me to get pregnant and begin acting like them."

Professional women also are often alienated from the men with whom they are supposed to assimilate. Kelly recalled that there were points in her career when the men she worked with were blatantly hostile. "When I first started at the auto company, the men used to steal work right off my desk. They didn't like the idea of me. If I went to lunch too long or I had a personal telephone call, they'd tell upper management. As I gained their confidence and respect, I overcame what they'd imposed on me, but it took a long time. It nearly drove me out of my mind."

Despite the obstacles, women have moved along, have excelled at their jobs and evolved into accomplished, self-confident people. But as women succeeded professionally, they discovered that their husbands' reactions weren't always as supportive as they'd promised they would be. "The husband begins to see his wife function in the workplace. He begins to observe her commitment to the job and feel that it interferes in some way with her role as wife. That's when the marriage becomes difficult. . . . The male begins to feel deficient. It becomes: you win, I lose. I think men, unfortunately, do feel diminished by female success," says Laurie Klein Evans, a family therapist and executive director of Canterbury Group Family Institute in Great Neck, New York.

"When women are professionally successful, they feel more self-confident," says Audrey Chapman, the family therapist. "They don't need as much affirmation from a man. They feel competent. Women need to be careful about how they project these feelings of competency or they may make men feel uncomfortable."

Some women who have accomplished their professional and economic goals may unwittingly bring their job personalities into their homes. The increased self-confidence that succeeding at a job engenders is expected in men in this society, not in women. Many husbands find it uncomfortable to live with a woman who appears to be their intellectual or financial equal. "There was a woman I was seeing in my practice, a really competent professional, who told me she was tired of being psyched out by men. What she was running into in dating were men who said to her in so many words, 'Listen, you know you don't identify with power and achievement. Let me see you as a sexy broad. You and I both know that's what you really are.' If we all think about it, women have traditionally been dependent on men for economic security. For women to be able to make money puts a new slant on the relationship."

As women began to earn money, they found they had clout their mothers never dreamed of. More important for others, however, was the sense of accomplishment and recognition that came purely from their work. "I produced a radio drama that won seventeen awards," said Rose, a radio producer. "The school system in my city used it. I was really proud of that." "I needed my job emotionally for the challenge and stimulation," said a nutritionist.

These working women declared that far from sharing their enthusiasm for their jobs, their husbands seemed to resent and feel jealous of their interest in work or in anything, for that matter, that took their wives' attention from them. That resentment sometimes came out in subtle ways. Rose said she was very hurt when her husband withheld praise for her accomplishment. "He just didn't say too much about the show. I think he knew I needed to hear some praise from him."

As increasingly self-possessed women began to be assertive and challenging at home, they found their mates chiding them to stop acting as though they were at work. The work personality—aggressive, driving, challenging—seems to be the antithesis of what many men want in a wife.

"My husband encouraged me to go to law school. He was very supportive of that," said Colleen, a business consultant from South Carolina. "But when I became involved in an extracurricular organization, that wasn't legitimate. My intelligence and assertiveness were okay as long as I applied them to issues he considered important. When it came to nurturing me on issues I considered important or just being responsive to me, that wasn't forthcoming from him."

Ambitious women who were learning the system were beginning to see the career advantages of high visibility. Many of them, however, report that their husbands are threatened when it appears wives may outdistance them publicly. Valerie, a university professor, told me about her husband's reaction when she became a campaign manager for a leading candidate for city office. "The most recent incident was that I stayed out with my campaign staff until midnight and didn't call. He had a right to be angry, but I feel it was a coverup for his true feelings about my working on the campaign. What he said after he got through railing about how I could have called was, 'Well, maybe you don't need to do this.' I think he wants me to get a little attention, but not too much."

As women earned more money and took on more responsibility in the workplace, they began to participate more actively in decision making at home. Many men saw themselves losing the privileges and power their fathers had been accorded. As the tables they'd agreed to turn spun around, they felt a disquieting array of emotions—fear of losing control, anger at being forced into uncomfortable changes. Many men began to feel they were giving up a lot— more than they were getting. "I do my share of the cooking and cleaning and what do I get?" one husband rhetorically asked. "I get a wife who spends most of her time working."

And unlike women, who found encouragement in consciousness-raising groups and other supports, men had no "movement" to turn to, no real understanding of their own oppressive socialization. "There may have been groups around the country calling for male liberation," says Dr. Alvin Poussaint, associate professor of psychiatry at the Harvard Medical School, "but many fewer than women's groups . . . The women's movement has a political component. There is no such component for men. I don't think men really perceive themselves as victims, because with the masculine characteristics come privilege and advantage."

Men who enthusiastically said "I do" to an egalitarian marriage soon discovered that their masculine advantage was being threatened by their new life-style. Though no one was saying it, some were suffering because of their difficulty in adjusting to an equal relationship. A recent study out of Rutgers University, conducted by Graham Staines, Deborah Fudge, and Kathleen Pottick, concludes that husbands of women who work experience less job and life satisfaction than men who are married to homemakers. The study found that regardless of the husband's age, income, or educational level, a wife's employment has a negative impact on a man's mental health. Researchers say this is true even in cases where men profess to feel positive about their wives' employment. One of the researchers concluded that men who have working wives still feel ultimately responsible for being good providers. It appears that the fact that their wives are working doesn't ease the man's emotional burden; rather, many men may feel guilty about receiving help to do something they have been socialized to feel is their sole responsibility. Researchers believe that instead of seeing their wives' financial contributions as positive, men brood over the fact that their own incomes aren't adequate to meet their families' financial needs.

Not all working women willingly undermine the male role of provider. Many employed women are traditionalists who are forced to work because of economic necessity and deeply resent having to do so. There are, of course, many men who are sole providers who may feel unduly burdened because they have to carry the entire financial weight of their families. "I don't meet a lot of men under age forty who seem so preoccupied with doing it all," says Michael Hughes, the therapist from Los Angeles. "I much more typically run into situations where a homemaker and a so-called traditional man separate and she gets a job. His response is, 'I wish she'd done that before.' Of course, he probably never voiced dissatisfaction about the money situation when they were married. For many couples, money is a very muddled issue."

Hughes says that lots of men are delighted that their partners earn money, particularly men who aren't overly ambitious or aggressive themselves. "There have always been men who are very readily inclined to get by with as little effort as possible. There are men who live off their wives. These aren't the average, but neither is the guy who shuts down because his wife earns money. In general, I think a woman doing well and bringing in significant income allows a man more freedom. It takes the pressure off him and lets him develop aspects of his behavior and particularly allows men to have a greater role in their children's lives."

Yet men are under pressure as they rise in their jobs. Men in the top echelons of corporations often are associating with older men who are married to traditional homemakers. These corporate leaders don't make allowances for career wives.

In addition, many men see their own peers with wives who are having babies and taking time off from work to care for them. The husband who is wavering in his own commitment to equality in his marriage is hard-pressed to find other men who encourage him to maintain a truly liberated stance. At the same time, working wives have trouble finding women who have totally or even largely given up the prerogative of choosing dependence when it's convenient. Still, since the boom of dual-career couples in the late 80s and 90s, married couples have many more options when they've hit a rough spot in their relationship, for example, support groups or couples therapy. Without such help, men and women struggle. Women say that in addition to all the job-related stresses they must contend with, the straw that breaks their backs is that their husbands also have become adversaries. On the other hand, men feel they aren't being supported and have the worst of all possible worlds as liberated husbands. What both want is a nurturing partner who will support their professional and emotional growth. Unable or unwilling to be open about their dissatisfactions, husbands and wives silently begin to try reshaping their spouses to accommodate their needs.

4

Do You Really Need Me?
The Fear Men Don't
Talk About

By the time many dual-career couples have been married for several years, the uneasy blending of old and new values has begun to strain their relationship. While working women have grown in self-confidence, with, according to a University of Michigan study, better mental health than full-time homemakers, increasingly husbands have been running into emotional difficulties in trying to "stay liberated."

Unfortunately their discomfort has overshadowed many of the personal gains they made in striving for equality in marriage. Those fledgling efforts—sharing the housework and cooking, taking care of children, supporting their wives' career aspirations—put many men in touch with feelings they didn't even know they had. Taking care of their children, they discovered their own ability to nurture. With their wives earning money, many are intensely relieved to be able to share the economic load. Some men are so joyful at being able to express emotions for the first time that, like Dr. Brod, they began raising their own consciousness.

Yet, many men reject this more flexible masculinity because of the anxiety it causes them. As they watch their wives succeed in their professions, they feel a nagging insecurity. John, the vice-president for a multinational energy company, put it succinctly, "I guess ultimately I believed that if my wife didn't need me for my money, she didn't need me."

Deep down, many men are afraid their independent wives will eventually abandon them. Taking care of women is so ingrained in their training that they see their wives' careers as a threat to their own ability to protect them from hostile outside forces. Because of their wives' independence husbands aren't supposed to protest late meetings, sexist bosses, overwork, and other men. They fear their silence will make them lose their wives' respect. Therefore many men turn their attention to holding back their women rather than continuing forward toward their own liberation.

Once men become disenchanted with egalitarian marriages, they are very clear about their objectives. "We'd had seven years of just the two of us and her career," explained an insurance executive. "I felt it was time for a more traditional life."

When that kind of pressure is applied, successful, independent women react by resisting. Far from retreating to subservience, they push for even more equality in their marriages and the situation can deteriorate rapidly. Persuading their wives to concentrate on motherhood seems an ideal way for many husbands to reaffirm their imperiled manhood. Men recently engaged began having second thoughts. One woman said, "When my husband and I agreed to get married I told him I wasn't sure I wanted children and he said that was fine with him. Now he's begun pressing for a child. When I say I'm not sure I want one, he says, 'What do you mean you may not want to have a child?' "

Men often begin setting the stage for reneging on their promise to share in child care even before their children are born. Said another woman, "When I became pregnant with our first child, I reminded my husband of our agreement to be equally involved in parenting. He kind of laughed and said, 'You know once the kid is born you're not going to let me do anything.' "

Barbara, a 36-year-old librarian, said, "I was really shocked when I discovered I was pregnant. It was the early seventies. My husband and I hadn't been married very long and we hadn't planned on having children for a while. Or at least I hadn't planned on having any." Barbara's unexpected pregnancy upset her, but she was stunned by her husband's reaction. It wasn't his joy at learning he was about to become a father; she'd expected that. What shocked her was the sudden abandonment of the principles upon which they'd founded their marriage. Along with a strong paternal instinct came a new view of his wife . . . and her place. In seeing himself as a father, Ralph began seeing Barbara as a mother—and his subordinate. "The first thing Ralph said to me was, 'You won't have to work.' And I remember thinking, What does he mean I won't have to work? I want to work. He knows that. What's he talking about?"

With her advancing pregnancy, it became very obvious to Barbara that her husband's plans were to scuttle their balanced relationship and replace it with a more traditional marriage, one in which she stayed home and took care of the baby while he made the money and all the decisions. Barbara wasn't interested in that kind of arrangement. "I couldn't envision myself staying at home taking care of a baby for any length of time. That's just not my makeup. I'm one of those women who is supposed to work."

Ralph disagreed and vehemently stressed that as the mother of their unborn child, she was best qualified to rear their baby. He pleaded with his wife that she stop working and not let some stranger take care of their child. That was the way it was supposed to be, Ralph told his wife.

Most men have grown up believing that women need babies to feel fulfilled. While they consider making a baby to be a powerful, manly act, after conception many men may feel they should detach from what they consider a totally feminine role: being a nurturer.

As men become more and more disenchanted with equality they gradually begin to neglect household chores. Women report finding the same men who had whipped up gourmet meals for several years and ironed to perfection, suddenly becoming helpless around the house. Others become forgetful about chores or too preoccupied: "My husband and I had agreed to split the housework and all of our expenses. He was supposed to do the washing, but he began to just let it pile up. I'd get exasperated and start to do it. Invariably, he'd stop me. He'd say he would do it later and suggest we leave the washing and do something that was fun instead."

"My husband started referring to his doing his share of the housework as *helping* me do my work. He wanted special praise for doing what we'd agreed upon," remarked another woman. At the same time, men say women begin to "weasel" out of doing man's work: mowing the lawn, driving for extended periods of time, and picking up the tab in restaurants.

Men also began to exhibit behavior that showed their disgruntlement with their wives' jobs. A number of women recalled husbands who began pressuring them to give less to their jobs and more to them. Said one, "He started asking me if I could come home from work earlier. When I had a real busy time at work and wasn't available to him, he told me I should think about getting another job."

"I began to notice there was competition in the conversations I'd have with my husband," Jennifer revealed. "We could talk for a long time about his work, his day, but when I started talking about mine, the topic got switched."

This changed attitude in the home was also taking place in the larger society. Men were having to compete with more women for executive positions and some of them brought their professional resentment home with them. As media images of the "first women to" flashed across the screen, many men began to feel that women—including their wives—were taking over. The backlash was evident in the defeat of ERA and the rise in the antiabortion movement. The growing conservatism was also felt in some homes. "If you women want so much equality, why don't you join the army?" It was suddenly in fashion to poke fun at feminist goals. As feminism began to be denigrated, some husbands even suggested their wives not associate with women they considered dangerous—that is, a feminist influence.

In response to their husbands many women became more fervently adamant about delaying childbirth or never having children. They responded to their husbands' negligence of housework, by going "on strike" or, if they could afford it, hiring housekeepers. And they had other ways of applying pressure in an attempt to change their husbands back to the liberated men they'd married.

"My husband and I had a lot of conversations about the women's movement," said an advertising executive from Los Angeles. "We went to all these lectures and heard a lot of speeches. One time we sat next to Gloria Steinem. But all the while, he was sort of scratching his head. He didn't believe any of it for a minute. He saw what he was going to lose."

Women report that they gave their husbands books and magazine articles on how they could become more liberated. They extolled husbands who fit the egalitarian definition and praised them not too subtly. They pointedly reminded their husbands about the chores they'd promised to do and compiled their own lists of dangerous men, that is to say, sexist men they wanted their husbands to avoid.

In the meantime, both partners were trying to keep up appearances and keep the marital difficulties they were experiencing from public view. In the closet, it was difficult to work things out. Men simply discarded the magazines and books without reading them. Career women simply continued to take their birth control pills and managed to delay the pregnancy they knew might result in a traditional straitjacket. Neither men nor women could confide in their friends because they were unwilling to admit even to themselves that something was going terribly wrong with their brave new marriages. Instead, they spent most of their energies trying to change each other into the person they'd fantasized they had married. Her reference point was the guy who said he would share her dreams of equality. What she forgot was that this man had not been told everything she expected and that the mixed signals she'd given him throughout their marriage had further confused and alienated him. His reference point was even more nebulous. He found it harder to make peace with the independent and persistent goals of the woman he married. They were each playing a different and separate game. Though they wanted to draw each other closer, the result was more and more distance between them—a wide-open space in which backlash found a place.

PART TWO

Backlash

5

Stage I: Male Criticism and the Emergence of Superwoman

In the beginning, Aurelia couldn't put her finger exactly on what was happening. She was so busy working and going to school she almost didn't notice her husband's subtle comments. Ken began complaining about little things. He told her the roast she'd prepared for Sunday dinner was tough. "Jesus Christ!" he'd said. "What is this mess? Moose meat?" It was almost funny; Aurelia remembered laughing a little, before catching herself when Ken stared coldly at her. Then, when she was dressing to go to work one morning not long after, Ken asked her why she wore her blue dress so often. "Don't you ever wear anything else?" he asked. "I'm getting sick of that thing." Aurelia was surprised by the irritation in his voice, far more than was warranted, she thought. "You always liked this dress," she said, carefully trying to monitor the hurt she felt. "I used to before you started wearing it every damn day," Ken retorted icily. Aurelia said nothing, but changed into a gray suit.

Maybe he's just having problems on the job, she thought, driving to the small social agency where she worked. Ken was an administrator of a community-based economic development program that always seemed to be in a funding crisis. He's just feeling irritable because we didn't make love last night, she decided on another occasion when Ken's critical observations seemed to come without provocation. After a while it seemed to Aurelia that nothing pleased him anymore. His comments persisted and even escalated in nastiness. Why had he become so hostile? What was wrong?

Then one evening when they were on their way to the home of friends, Ken told Aurelia that her hair didn't look right, that it never looked right anymore. His caustic remark was par for the course, but his postscript struck Aurelia. "I guess lawyers don't care what their hair looks like, huh?"

Aurelia thought it was a strange comment. What did being a lawyer have to do with how she wore her hair? Besides, she wasn't a lawyer, she'd only begun law school a few months before. He couldn't be upset about that, she thought. He's the one who encouraged me to go. Sure, he had warned her that her studies would be difficult and time-consuming and that studying for the bar would be exhausting, but she knew Ken was always cautious. Yet, something about Ken's tone, the way he spat out the word *lawyer,* stayed with her.

Why had he said that in such a mean way? Aurelia pushed away those disturbing thoughts and instead examined herself in the mirror, assessing her hair, her face, her figure and skin, all the elements of herself her husband had once loved and now seemingly didn't. Yes, that was the problem, she thought with a sigh of relief. Maybe she wasn't as attractive as she used to be.

Ken's longing for Aurelia came out sounding angry. Ken never really accepted his wife's return to school, but he didn't know how to express his disapproval, since it was initiated by feelings he'd always repressed—feelings of need and dependency. Most men who criticize hope their wives will somehow see through their criticism and realize without their having to verbally communicate it that they want more attention, companionship, and devotion. When his hints and silence were seemingly ignored, and the reality of Aurelia's decision to pursue a law degree hit home, his anger and criticism escalated.

Aurelia's response was to goad herself from one task to another in a perpetual frantic state. She never seemed to get angry but, instead, submerged the twinges of resentment that cropped up when she felt Ken was being demanding and unfair. When she was confronted with Ken's hostile criticism, she submitted, hoping it would disappear. But it didn't.

Neither Ken nor Aurelia realized it, but their marriage had entered what my research reveals is present in many families as the first stage of backlash, when men criticize and pick on their wives.[18] They do this as a way to express disapproval and to manipulate women emotionally into being more dependent and subservient. Criticism is the first wave of emotional release that men who are uncomfortable with their wives' professional status allow themselves. It is the first overtly hostile act that husbands make in an attempt to change how their professional wives relate to them. Implicit in this hostility is the male's attempt to regain power he feels he's lost by virtue of his wife's professional status and accompanying independence. By subtly "putting down" their wives, husbands have an outlet for their anger and they avoid a troubling revelation: admitting they are uncomfortable with an equal relationship.

Criticism doesn't occur by itself. It is often accompanied by men becoming increasingly hostile, attempting to make their wives more emotionally dependent, and refusing to do housework. Women don't want to talk about their husbands' discomfort or theirs either. The female reaction to backlash, for the most part, is a fearful avoidance of the issue. Instead of facing it, women plunge into the role of superwoman, attempting to do a superlative job at home and on the job. They work themselves into a frenzy, trying to be above reproach.

People in crumbling relationships often criticize each

---

[18] Audrey Chapman, the therapist, first advanced the theory of the first and subsequent stages of backlash.

other, but from what the respondents have said, the basis of backlash criticism is the male's need to feel secure that his wife loves and needs him and will not abandon him. The aim is to pressure the woman into retreating from her professional aspirations and elevating the role of wife to the paramount one in her life. By criticizing wives for not acting in a traditional manner, men hope to distance themselves from the equality that they have found to be so uncomfortable. *In other words, the purpose of criticism in backlash isn't so much to correct female behavior, as to reestablish male dominance and undermine sexual equality in the marriage.*

From what I've observed across the country, it is important that working men and women be able to identify and interpret this first stage accurately, because at this early point, it is still possible to save the marriage. The problem is difficult because backlash criticism is hidden behind a disquieting array of conflicting male emotions. It may take even the most perceptive wife a while to understand the incentive for the psychological warfare her husband is engaging in.

For example, Donna, 34, a manager for a large corporation in Philadelphia, hadn't a clue as to why her long-term live-in lover suddenly began to pick her apart. She vaguely felt that their troubles began when she finished graduate school and began working on a senator's campaign, but she never thought that George, 36, a city planner, might resent her career. He seemed far too supportive. Yet, from a warm, loving partner, he began turning into a nag. "He was constantly on me about every little thing. He'd say, 'I don't like what you're wearing; it makes you look fat.' 'Hurry up, you're going too slow.' 'You're so clumsy,' " Donna said.

Then one night when she and George were dining out, he did something Donna couldn't ignore. "His father, step-mother, two sisters, George, and I all went out to this very nice restaurant. When the waiter brought the check, George picked up the tab for everyone, then he turned to me and said, 'You're working. You're a big-time professional woman. Why don't you pay for your own dinner?' I was flabbergasted," recalled Donna.

She was also out of the dark about what was going on in her relationship. It was the first time George had mentioned anything specific about her job in a resentful way, but Donna began to pick up other clues. "He'd say things like, 'You're always so busy.' Or he'd call me on the job at five and de-mand that I be ready to leave in ten minutes. And," Donna added with a sigh, "he stopped helping me with the house-work."

Men abandoning household responsibilities is a common early warning signal in the first stage of backlash. Unlike the playful negligence of chores in prebacklash days, in the first stage of backlash men are deliberately hostile in their refusal to do chores they agreed to. "When I got married, it was supposed to be fifty-fifty, and for a while it seemed to be that way," said Alice, 29, a fashion designer with a prestigious firm in New York City. Her husband Phillip, 29, a hospital administrator, earns much less than the nearly $40,000 that

Alice brings home. The mother of a one-year-old daughter, Alice said that since her baby's birth, her husband has been criticizing her more and more and revealing that he resents her job and superior salary. "There was a time when if he dirtied the dishes, he'd wash them. Now he just leaves the plates in the sink. Instead of putting his clothes in the hamper, he now puts them on top of it. That's ridiculous. He never did this before," Alice declared. "Why is he changing?"

Wayne, the owner of an independent insurance agency, admitted that he stopped cleaning and cooking, household chores he'd always done, once his wife, a tenured professor at a large university, began working long hours and expanding her community commitments. "My wife leaves the house around seven in the morning and I don't see her again until around nine o'clock at night. I'm not happy about that and I've told her as much. She hasn't changed, so I guess my attitude has been, 'Hey, if you're not going to be there for me, I'm not going to help you with this house.' "

Men say their wives' perfectionist housekeeping standards often discourage them from pitching in at home. Women put down their husbands' early attempts at "helping." While Wayne admits that he doesn't do housework because he resents his wife's neglect, he also maintains that his wife didn't show appreciation when he did clean the house. "First of all, I never did the chores right, according to her. My wife is a perfectionist. She used to go back and redo everything that I'd done."

Working women, reared above all else to be "good little housewives," often have the same standards of homemaking that their housebound mothers had. While there are many men who are neater than women and far more fastidious as cleaners, for many years, women acquired a sense of high self-esteem through maintaining a neat, well-decorated home, the same sense of well-being that a man acquired through his work. The driven, perfectionist woman who has high professional goals may well be likely to include the condition of her home as part of her sense of self-worth. Even though she works, her identity is still bound by the compulsion to be a good homemaker. Instead of feeling appreciative of her husband's attempts and encouraging her mate to do more through praise, she antagonizes and ultimately turns him off by criticizing him for failing to meet the white-glove standards that reflect positively upon her. In some instances, women sabotage their men's efforts because they really don't want to share their domestic autonomy, they want to be in charge of their homes just like traditional women. Some women make the mistake of constantly comparing their husbands' cleaning, childcare, and cooking, with what other men do. Others clean up behind their men, who, in view of their own ambivalence, don't need much of an excuse to stop doing their share.

Wayne felt justified in reacting negatively to a wife he believed wasn't considering his needs at all. Like many of the husbands I spoke with, Wayne feels his wife is so locked into her career track that she is unwilling to veer from it to allow space for growth in their relationship. His wife Crystal admitted that her job, community service, and the various boards that she serves on take up most of her week and that she didn't see herself making any changes in the foreseeable future. Crystal knows that her husband wants more attention from her, but she is blunt about the things she isn't willing to do. "It hit Wayne about three years ago that I was gone a lot. He told me, 'I never see you. You're always on the road. I'm beginning to lose weight because nobody cooks for me.' Well, I am on the road a lot, but even if I weren't, I wouldn't cook six meals a week. I cooked from the time I was nine years old.

"He's not willing to compromise," said Crystal. "He expects me to change my schedule so that we can spend more time together, while he never wants to change his basketball date with the boys."

The professor believes she has supported her husband in the best way she can. "He said, 'I need you to push me.' I've done that," Crystal declared vehemently. "I've provided him with the financial support so he could go search for his rainbow," she said. "Most of his clients come from my contacts." She declares that more time is the one thing she can't give him.

The difficulty of juggling many roles plagues working women early in their marriages, but as their careers demand more and more energy, the pressures mount. They haven't learned to limit the energy they give to their jobs and outside interests so they have something left for their personal lives.

In many cases, they have sacrificed their personal lives to the goal of independence and self-fulfillment. Other women are trapped by work styles that engulf them against their wills. They emulate the same men they declare are their oppressors: those who work late, compete hard, and give only 2 percent of themselves to their families.

Resentful husbands, anxious to be dominant in their partners' lives, exert psychological pressure on vulnerable wives. Reacting to the fear of not being needed, men attempt to establish their importance and dominance in their wives' lives by asserting that the woman who seeks independence and success in a career is lacking in some fundamental way. "My husband used to tell me I couldn't survive without him," said Helen, an architect from California, who echoed many of the women I interviewed.

When more aggressive professional women take the stance that a real feminist doesn't negotiate or compromise her equality, subtle domestic warfare escalates. Unwilling to work through the inevitable problems that arise when people break away from traditional social patterns, many professional women issue ultimatums to their husbands.

"I can't forget the day my wife sat down and drew up a contract for the housework and taking care of the children," said Martin, 40, a Washington writer, in an outraged tone of voice. "She wrote down everything that I was supposed to do. One of my chores was cleaning the oven, and God, I hated that. There was a commercial on at the time that showed a woman bending over cleaning an oven. Everything on her list I associated with women, and I resisted being locked into these female chores. I did everything under protest and finally I just quit doing anything. I used to feel that she was cracking a whip and I hated that feeling."

Taking orders from their wives is hard for men who were brought up to believe a real man controls his woman and that most women expect and want masculine dominance. Men say they are bewildered. "What do women want?" they ask.

In the July 1985 issue of *Essence* magazine, Donald Singletary wrote about the confusion of men attempting to decipher those kinds of mixed messages from women.

In the last few years—since women began their quest for greater personal independence, better jobs and pay comparable to men's and the right to make decisions about what they do with their bodies—men have struggled to understand this "new woman." The signals that we are getting are that women want to take charge of their own destinies. They want to compete alongside men for the fruits of success in society. They no longer wish to rely on men for the things that they want out of life. Instead, they have opted to get it themselves. Although these changes do in fact create some anxiety among men, many feel that they will ultimately free men from some of the traditional male responsibilities society has imposed upon them. Ideally, this should mean men no longer have to carry the full burden of financial support, decision making and being the aggressor in romantic pursuits. Right?

Wrong! That's one message women send. But there is another message that says, "I'll have my cake and eat yours too."

According to Singletary and others, the traditional male value system has been kept alive by women just as much, if not more than, by men. Women are unwilling to entirely abandon the ideal of the traditional marriage that says men must be breadwinners. And they communicate their belief in this unbalanced financial responsibility to their husbands in no uncertain terms. Many women assume they can drop out of the workforce whenever and for as long as they choose, particularly if they decide to have children. In contrast, women are visibly uncomfortable with men who depend upon their financial assistance. Most women don't encourage their husbands to feel they have an equal right to take time out from work to care for children, go to school, or just take a much needed break. One woman whose husband had quit his job to go out on his own admitted her resentment at his lack of earning power and her position as the family breadwinner. "I don't like having to take care of a man," she said. Yet, she confessed she would have no qualms about a reverse situation. Moreover, most single professional women readily admit that in choosing prospective mates, their preference is to marry a man who makes as much or more money than they do. Several working wives, who claimed to want fifty-fifty marriages, went even further and declared they liked "strong" men as opposed to weak. They defined male strength as being decisive and taking charge.

Men accuse women of being reluctant to relinquish 50 percent of the parental responsibility they have been socialized to accept as their role. Women feel they have carried the child for nine months, nursed it, and find that despite feminist persuasion, they aren't prepared to share the basic authority for the child. Men speak of being locked out of their children's lives by women who want full control of their offspring. Men accuse women of making them feel inept as parents when their wives berate their attempts to braid hair, dress, bathe, or feed their children. "I always felt that I didn't get adequate exposure to my son," Jim, 41, a federal government executive told me. "I wanted to spend some time with him by myself. My wife wanted to take the baby with her everywhere she wanted to go, but I couldn't take him everywhere I wanted to go. Her girlfriends spent more time with the baby than I did."

Yet many women declare they are more than willing to relinquish their sole rights to shape and mold their children. They welcome male support, but have trouble getting it. "My husband and I do split the responsibility for our five-year-old daughter," said Linda, "and he's not altogether happy about having the responsibility. He's been able to verbalize that. He is absolutely appalled at what equal responsibility for a child means."

As male frustration increases, so does backlash. When I visited Melva, 35, a physician, and her husband Herb, an engineer, in their Virginia home, they both agreed that there was no backlash in their own relationship. "He's always supported me all the way," Melva declared as Herb quietly smiled. "He does more than his share of the housework and childcare. He's far more nurturing of our daughter than I am." Melva was proud of her husband's egalitarianism and grateful for it. She had a friend who wasn't so fortunate.

"There's one couple I know where the husband is a perfect example of backlash. The wife is a dentist and went to dental school during their marriage, a move that he claimed to support. But I believe he's always had a lot of conflicts about her being a dentist. He wants the good life, but he also wants her to be an earth mother who caters to his every whim. I've watched him ever since they got married, ten years ago, and I can see the difference her being a dentist has made. He resents the fact that she is the greater wage earner and he shows it by being really mean to her when they're around other people. He criticizes everything she does, puts her down in every way he can. He even curses at her in front of people in a nasty, belittling way. God knows what goes on when they're alone."

Men also claim that they are criticized in public by women who poke fun at their efforts to take on nontraditional roles. Women insist far more men find fault with their wives for not doing "traditional" women's work or not doing it consistently well. Women are resentful when it becomes apparent that what they believed to be their husband's commitment to sharing household work was actually the male belief that they were "helping" their wives do "women's work."

The physical toll of working, maintaining a home, and taking care of children begins to wear women out. Some reluctantly drop standards of perfectionist cleanliness that they inherited from their mothers. Most don't drop the standards, just the ability to maintain them. Those who can afford to, try to hire domestic help, although this isn't always an easy remedy. Many men resist getting outside help, because they feel doing household tasks represents a woman's love for her family. Some women abstain from hiring maids for the same reason. Those who can afford maids and employ them often find that some husbands have no qualms about criticizing help hired to act out the wife's role.

"I finally hired a cleaning lady because I was working a lot and I could see that my husband and daughters weren't going to take up the slack," said Wanda, a news reporter from a large midwestern town. "We must have gone through six or seven cleaning ladies in a year. My husband would always find some reason the woman wasn't working out. I'd come home and he'd say, 'Oh, hi, darling, I want to show you something.' Then he'd take me from room to room and show me what the cleaning lady hadn't done. Although he never said so, it was obvious from his constant criticism that he wanted me to be the hands-on person who took care of the household. I think he equated my taking care of the house and keeping it clean with my loving him."

Beatrice's resentment grew as it became apparent that no

area of her life was sacred as far as her husband's critical eye was concerned. While the university professor admitted to herself that she wasn't the best housekeeper and cook and that perhaps her husband did have grounds for complaint, her guard went up when her husband began to make negative comments about her work. "When I started teaching at my previous university, my career really shot off. I became supercreative. I got awards for my teaching. During this time, I wrote a paper in order to qualify for an overseas conference and after I finished writing it, I asked my husband for his comments. Well, he read it and proceeded to write all over it," said Beatrice with an amused expression on her face. "He told me, 'I'll tell you honestly, I wouldn't accept this if you were my best friend.' " Beatrice laughed out loud. She told me the paper was accepted and she went on the trip. She said, "He was trying to attack me on a level where I was pretty proficient. The irony was that in the past, I had helped him to write things and he had always complimented me. Of course, that's because then my work benefited him."

While the dual-career marriage seethes from within, it is assailed by criticism from outside too, although dual-career families comprised 60 percent of all marriages in 1996.[19] Neither men nor women receive full support from friends and relatives for trying to work out a nontraditional marriage. Snide or well-intentioned remarks from outsiders can

---

[19] From Catalyst.

further wound a fragile relationship. Men face censorship from relatives and friends for being liberated. "When my father found out that I was cooking and washing dishes, he had a fit," confided John, with a slight grin. "He told me, 'Son, you're doing too much. That's the woman's job.' "

"My husband has a friend who has said to him 'Man, you should make your wife stop all that traveling,' " said Crystal.

Other women, especially mothers and sisters-in-law, criticize professional women because they feel an allegiance to the husband or to warn a working wife that she must be more accommodating if she wants to remain married. There are times when other women are envious of the professional woman's independence and criticize her to knock her down a peg or two.

"My mother wishes that I were more domestic," said Susan, 37, a business consultant from Atlanta. "She figures that I neglect my husband. She tells me, 'You don't cook enough. You should fix up the house.' "

"Herb's sisters are nurturing and they don't see that in me," said Melva, the physician. "One of them told me that I didn't keep my daughter's shoes clean enough when she was a baby."

Melva says the snide remarks of her sisters-in-law pale in comparison with the criticism she receives from the practical nurses on whom she is forced to depend. "Most of the female doctors I know have power struggles with the practical nurses. The male doctors snap their fingers and they have everything they need. Female doctors have to call for a practical nurse two or three times before they show up. They're always slower in responding to us. Then when you're alone with them, they make little remarks like, 'Gee, you work until eight P.M. Goodness, who picks up your kid?' or 'Gee, aren't you afraid for your little girl to ride the school bus, all those accidents and everything?' One of them said to me last week, 'Say, honey, what are you going to do when you start making all that big money? Do you think that your husband is going to stay with you? Aren't you scared that he's going to give your money to another woman? Probably someone just like me, who knows how to treat a man.' Do you believe that?" Melva asked.

While most of the pressure men face from outsiders stems from males who criticize them for being too liberated, occasionally they are told the same things by women. "When my wife and I opted to have our child the Lamaze way, which meant I'd coach her through labor, both my mother and mother-in-law criticized me. They told me that was the woman's job," said Jim. On the other side of the coin, wives grumble that their husbands are applauded, particularly by women, for every dish they wash, while it is assumed that women do the housework.

It's evident that in attempting to forge a new kind of marriage, both men and women are suffering, but women claim they are overwhelmed by their load. The childcare and housework that a husband begins to shuck off as he comes to grips with his anger fall directly on the overburdened shoulders of working wives. As she attempts to be a full-time homemaker and professional, the wife strives to be super-woman. To balance all her roles, her day is filled with endless obligations.

It feels awful, these women declare. "There are days when I feel like screaming," said Margaret, the manager from Denver. "I have to tell my husband over and over, 'Look, I'm not the only one who sleeps in this bed. You make it sometimes.' At work, I have to go full steam all day long. Then I come home and I'm on duty all over again. Not long ago my husband and I and another couple decided to go on a picnic. The other wife and I had to do everything. We had to buy the food, prepare it, pack it. By the time everything was ready, we were too tired to go anywhere. Of course, the men were raring to go."

"It got to be crazy," said Aurelia about her superwoman experience. "Every day I thought I was going to lose my mind. First of all, I was working and still had a full caseload of clients. Then, there was law school and all the reading and assignments and study sessions that I had to do for that. Then, when Ken began complaining about everything, I was running around trying to make sure that the house was spick-and-span, that I was gorgeous, and everything was just perfect. I began going perfectly nuts."

The frenetic pace begins to take a toll. Audrey Chapman, the therapist and human relations trainer in Washington D.C., who specializes in stress management seminars for female professionals, says many of her patients exhibit what she calls the aftereffects of the superwoman syndrome. "I see a high rate of alcoholism and cocaine and marijuana abuse. Lots of tranquilizers. The women exhibit a lot of psychosomatic pain in their backs and necks. They have severe menstrual cramps. The pain isn't as much physical as it is mental. The stress leads to other more serious ailments."

By burying themselves in work, some women escape coming to grips with their growing resentment at being "dumped on" by men on the job and at home. Others take on the role of superwoman without complaining because they are convinced that it is a normal situation. Television commercials flash across the screen images of the sophisticated, slick-suited Madison Avenue businesswoman, wheeling and dealing with briefcase in hand by day and casually whipping up a gourmet dinner in a sexy frock, transformed from career woman to glamorous wife and mother by a quick spritz of perfume. The media has so normalized the image of the woman performing superlatively on all fronts that average women hesitate to reveal that they feel overworked, that they are about to faint from fatigue. Society is telling them that if they can't do everything, somehow, they don't quite measure up and aren't worthy of "having it all." For the masses of working women who can't keep up the frenzied tempo, the imprint of their earlier socialization leads to guilty feelings for leaving small children or failing to do all the things that "good" wives do for their husbands.

Others feel Madison Avenue is less to blame for their stress than is the traditional upbringing they and men have had and can't detach from. "I struggle now with my ambition and my role of mother," said Kim, a clinical psychologist from North Carolina. "I feel a responsibility to be emotionally available to my five-year-old daughter. I wasn't there for her first day of school last year, because I was starting a new job. That was major guilt. My husband was there to take up the slack, but I still felt bad. I've been in private practice for four years and I also teach. My husband was completely for it. He's been extremely supportive of my career. He encouraged my private practice, but his encouragement was on an intellectual level. When it gets down to the time I'm going to be home and that I'm going to be tired when I get there—that's a different issue. A lot of men I've come in contact with, intellectually can support the feminist movement and equality in the relationship. They encourage their spouses to be successful career women. But on an emotional level it's much harder, because they never really understand the impact of what that means in real life situations. It means men will have to make their own dinners. That's right, honey, go into the refrigerator and look for food. And I guess what women didn't realize is that we've been so programmed to do all that stuff that when we don't, we feel tremendously guilty."

As the load piles up women become more and more frustrated as they balance fatigue, their husband's resentment, and their own guilt. Some women will remain trapped between their to-do lists for years, never knowing where their joy and zest for life went. The fatigue of covering too many fronts will cause a few to make a hasty retreat to more peaceful full-time domesticity, but faced with economic realities, most couples cannot afford to have the wife become a full-time homemaker.

Ultimately, the superwoman syndrome comes back to haunt the men who not only have helped to perpetuate it, but who seemingly stand to gain the most from it. The more husbands criticize their wives, the more frustrated the women become, distancing themselves even further from their spouses. By the time men realize that they don't want their wives to do the dishes and cook as much as they want them to pay attention to them by being closer and more loving, it may be too late. Women have begun to use the only escape hatch provided to avoid closeness and communication with the husbands they've begun to resent: they are staying at work as late as they possibly can and cooking the next day's dinner after midnight. They are retreating from their relationships behind a superwoman syndrome that is making them angrier and angrier even as they burn out.

6

Stage II: Angry Men, Burnt-Out Women

The night of the television awards ceremony was to be the happiest, proudest moment in Sylvia's career. Her work as a producer of a popular local talk show had garnered her considerable recognition and the industry's highest honor. Yet, three years later, when she recalled the ceremony, what stood out in her mind was not the pride she felt in accepting the award or the tumultuous applause, or the chorus of congratulations. What came to mind was her husband's angry, snarling response to her professional victory. What Sylvia remembers best about that night was the meanness in her husband's eyes.

Until that night, her husband Bob had publicly praised every promotion she'd received and had bragged about her prestigious career to friends and colleagues. "I would meet his co-workers and they'd say, 'Oh, your husband's so proud of you. He's always telling us what you're up to.' " That had been his public "front," as Sylvia liked to call it. In private, she knew that he had difficulties accepting a career that put her in the spotlight and him, a former entertainer turned financial consultant, in the background. She'd learned to underplay what she did, to preserve his ego and avoid fights. If people came up to both of them, raving about her show, she would cut them off by saying that she didn't want to discuss work, even though, secretly, she loved the praise and the response.

Trying to stay in her husband's shadow when she cast such a large one herself was impossible. And the more she shone, the more he resented her. In the beginning, that resentment came out in criticism. Then the criticism took a nasty turn. "He used to tell me that I had such big feet that he had to call me Bam Bam. Then he began calling me Horseface. He constantly said that I was fat and dowdy," Sylvia recalled. Then Bob became even more hostile. She recalled the night they had a party and Sylvia had been particularly opinionated; he'd cornered her in the kitchen, grabbing her hard by her arm, and said, "You're such a smart bitch. You think you know so much."

Sylvia knew that she had trouble, but until the awards ceremony, she wasn't aware of how resentful her husband was. On that night he dropped his public front of being the adoring, supportive, liberated husband and turned on her in a calculated attempt to sabotage her moment of glory.

"We traveled out of town for the awards presentation," she recalled. "The show's staff and all the spouses were staying in a fancy hotel, and everything was really plush. Bob likes traveling and he likes nice things, but on this trip he was very subdued."

The ceremony took place at a hotel ballroom. Sylvia and her staff were seated near the podium; the assembled spouses were at tables several feet away. When the emcee presented the award to Sylvia's group, she looked toward her husband and smiled. Then she returned to the table with her co-workers.

"Later, after the program, I made my way back to my husband," Sylvia continued. "I was so elated, so happy, and I wanted to share my big moment with him. The first thing he said to me was, 'Why didn't you come and kiss me?' He was enraged because I hadn't walked from the stage to his table to give him a kiss." "You didn't make me a part of this," he accused Sylvia. "I tried to explain to him that it would have been awkward. In a cold voice he told me he was taking the plane back that evening. Then he turned away from me. Meanwhile, we were standing in the middle of the ballroom floor. People were coming up to congratulate me. There I was surrounded by major executives, trying to chat with the president of the company, and my husband wouldn't speak to me. I was so upset, so completely out of control that I had to excuse myself so that I could go and throw up."

The second stage of backlash is an outpouring of rage

from men who cease expressing their dissatisfaction in vague criticism and become blatantly hostile over clear-cut issues. "I don't like that dress," becomes, "If you didn't stay out half the night going to so many damn meetings, maybe you'd have time for me once in awhile." Along with the rage comes rejection of feminist values, which may have been tolerated or even accepted earlier in the marriage. Both men and women I spoke with say this period reflects the deep-seated anger that has festered while men watch their superwomen move even further away from them. Husbands shout that they get their wives' leftover time, leftover enthusiasm, and leftover attention. The job, they assert, comes first with these women who have become so businesslike they've lost their warmth and femininity. They would rather work than be mothers, wives, lovers. Men complain that self-centered women have abused equality. Feeling used, formerly liberated men turn mean and try to force their wives to give them the devotion and loyalty they want. They say that if they act like men, real men, instead of wimps, their wives will have to start acting like real women.

If men sublimate their rage in the first stage of backlash, in the second they unleash it, vehemently expressing their resentment toward their wives' bosses, co-workers, her promotions and credentials. As male hostility escalates, husbands begin to sabotage their wives' careers in an effort to minimize and even destroy the vehicle of her independence. Wives react defensively, trying to cope with their husbands' sudden temper tantrums. Women become even more stressed as their biological clocks tick away and men once again press for a child in the hopes it will make their wives more dependent upon them. If they already have children they angrily renege on childcare responsibilities. As males demand the kinds of traditional power and female-delivered services their fathers enjoyed, women become overwhelmed. Harried by guilt, emotional and physical fatigue, and even poor health, perceiving themselves to be failing in all their roles, they begin to burn out. The sexual malaise of women who are too exhausted and gradually too resentful to make love distances couples even further and forces many women to come to grips with their own growing rage.

Society makes it difficult for men with working wives not to feel cheated. As backlash escalates, traditional corporate culture may work against egalitarian marriages. Women not only have to contend with men who are geared toward being traditional, but also with the institutions that still support male dominance.

While corporations have opened their doors to women, most don't actively support the dual-career couple. Careers are short-circuited if employees are unable to make long-distance moves, a common problem when two careers are involved. Most companies certainly don't take into consideration the childcare situation when both parents work.

When the busy schedules of working couples get crossed, companies expect the man to make sure that his wife defers to his career. Sometimes spouses are required to be present at corporate activities and functions. Those men whose wives aren't present because they are busy managing their own careers are penalized for not being able to control their wives. "When the company gives a function and the boss makes it clear that wives are to be present, if your wife doesn't show up, it hurts you. The upper management will figure out a way to stick it to you somewhere down the line. That's part of following orders," said Rick, an employment counselor. "You see, if the company puts on a dog-and-pony show, trying to convince a client that our company stands for solid American values, the little woman is part of the package."

"On James's last job, I missed quite a few of his functions because they conflicted with my schedule," Jennifer admitted. "His district and regional managers were older men who had real problems with my absence. They mentioned their feelings to him. Then James came home and said, 'Well, if you could show up, it would be nice.' " Jennifer feels that her husband's job promotes backlash. She says that his superiors view his inability to control his wife as a professional flaw, a general inability to manage on the job. Indeed, the stereotype of the consummate corporate executive includes a wife who stays at home. The arrangement presupposes that there is one life—the husband's—and that the female is augmenting that life. Because corporations uphold and reward traditional families, formerly egalitarian men, anxious to succeed on the job, begin to see the advantages of a wife who is a homemaker.

"I understand why successful men have had more than one wife. I've considered separation and divorce, but we've spent too many years together to walk out," said one man who worked as a pharmacist. "If I did remarry, I wouldn't want another woman like my wife. With someone else I'd have to be the center of attention. Men have very fragile egos and I'm no different. I need confirmation."

"The traditional woman does seem attractive to me," said Donald, a CPA from Atlanta, who's married to Susan, the business consultant. "I don't know if I'd choose a career woman again. I see now that I'm more the traditional type. I think the woman should have a career, but maybe something that runs nine to five. With every career there are other responsibilities in the relationship. You have to divorce that career from those other responsibilities. One of them is being around when someone else needs you."

And professional women admit they don't always know what they want from men, giving the excuse that they are still trying on for size success and all of its trappings. They say their work roles are so new they don't know everything they'll need from a spouse in terms of support. While some are exhilarated by their professional responsibilities, many say they are stunned by the personal cost of success: lack of time with their families, having to delay having children or limit the time spent with them, a schedule that prohibits personal development. Many have no role models for independence other than their fathers and other prominent males in their life. If they don't know what kind of masculine expression they want from their husbands, they are often equally unsure of how feminine they can afford to be as working women. As their careers mature, they are under increasing pressure at work to become a "macho female." This powerful, assertive woman is often threatening and unattractive to husbands.

"My wife's personality has changed," said Donald quietly when I was with him and his wife Susan in their Atlanta home. "You can tell that she's been around a lot of males—in an environment where there is free exchange of language. I consider her cursing unfeminine."

That Susan has decided for herself the language she is going to use, rather than abiding by prescribed guidelines of feminine behavior, may be even more of an affront to her husband than her cursing. Women who no longer ask their husbands' opinion on the clothes they wear, how they should act at work, or on personal business matters, who make their own decisions without consulting their husbands frighten many men.

Those fears may be connected to their subconscious belief in the old idea that women are either dependent and pure or independent and wicked and that a powerful woman will use her strength to a man's detriment. In traditional marriages the potentially bad woman is controlled by economic dependency. Husbands of professional wives don't have such authority, though often they wish they did. An insecure husband may attempt to erode a wife's self-confidence by negating her self-worth with putdowns and accusations. "My husband tried to undermine my self-confidence," said Sue, an executive director of a community center in the Midwest.

"He would constantly tell me that I'm such a strong personality that people can't get along with me. For a while I dismissed his comments, but gradually I began to doubt myself. When I'd have conflicts with people, his criticism would nag at me. I found myself second guessing myself more than I should have."

For a man's wife to be in charge of him can be an insuperable assault to his ego, striking at the heart of his traditional sense of macho. Cheryl, 30, a systems analyst at a computer firm outside of Washington, D.C., says that from the beginning, she and her husband, a cameraman at a local television station, knew that she would be the superior wage earner. "I had a graduate degree and he didn't and I'd made the decision to go into the private sector," she explained. Although her husband declared that he didn't mind her earning more that he did, he began to resent the fact that Cheryl handled the family finances and would often veto what she thought were his frivolous spending ideas. She said, "He didn't have the financial freedom he wanted and when he didn't get what he wanted, he would become angry." According to Cheryl, her husband tried to make their home a place where he exerted full control of the decision making outside of the family finances. "Sometimes if he wanted to do something and I didn't, he'd scream at me, 'There's not going to be any discussion. I've decided what we're going to do.' " Cheryl said that her husband accused her of not being a good wife because of her businesslike attitude. "Sometimes if I came home, keyed up from work, and I told him to do something, he'd say, 'You better turn off that work stuff. I'm not someone you're supervising.' " The analyst admitted that sometimes she was overbearing. "It's true. There have been times that I've had trouble shifting gears and I'd treat him like someone I was managing."

Even with cries of mea culpa, women are quick to point out that males have brought home their work attitudes for years, dictating most decisions about everyday life-styles to their wives. Women say they are expected to become sub-servient when they leave jobs where they are rewarded for acting independently. They say that switching assertiveness on and off leaves them stressed. They want men who appre-ciate their intellect, as well as their ability to serve dinner. Many men openly admit that the main thing they want from their wives isn't intellectual stimulation. What they want is affirmation and pride in their masculine power. "I needed a completer, not a competer," said the energy firm executive succinctly.

Ted, an engineer, clarified his needs even further. "Flo says in public that I'm the boss. I like that because of my chau-vinistic upbringing. I don't mind Flo making some routine decisions; however, when it comes down to certain confrontations that can happen in a household, I want my wife to turn to me, look for the answer from me. When a fourteen-year-old with a pistol comes charging through the door saying, 'Give me your dough or you're dead,' I want to know from my wife's perspective that I'm the leader. Only if I know that I'm the leader in her sight will I take the first step to smash that son-of-a-bitch. I need to know that I'm the strength of the house."

His wife, an elected official, admits that she likes to feel protected and that she gets that secure feeling from her mate. Yet, Flo doesn't want to have to act in what she considers a subservient manner to elicit his protection. The dilemma facing the marriage is that Ted claims that only if his wife acts in a more traditional manner will he have the ego gratification he needs to be her protector. As Flo and Ted grapple with new and old roles, the hostility level in their marriage rises.

During the second stage, men begin to strike out directly at their wives' jobs. Some women report that instead of the support they promised to give, husbands are attacking all the professional progress they make and creating a tense atmosphere where achievement is difficult. Alice, the designer from New York, shared with me an encounter with her husband that unnerved her. "I brought home a stack of papers from the computer for my little girl to draw on. While I was taking it out, my husband came into her room. He gave me this really strange, angry look and said, 'What's that, another award?' I mean, the way he said it, so mean and sarcastic," Alice said, stressing her husband's tone with a gesture of her hand. "Sure I get awards; it's the nature of my job. They're no big deal. I usually just leave them at the office. I think that a couple of times I've brought them home. He never praised me when I did." Alice claimed that her husband resents her upward mobility but wants the financial rewards it brings. When she turned down a recent promotion that would have meant a $10,000 raise, he was angry.

Beatrice, the professor from North Carolina, recalled that her husband became enraged when she would question his decisions. He used to tell her, "You think you know so much because you have a Ph.D." "It got to a point in our marriage where I couldn't talk with my husband about what I was doing at work. He wouldn't respond at all," said Helen, the architect.

Looking back, Donna realizes that the more her job demanded of her, the angrier George became. "He used to call my office and demand that the secretaries interrupt my meetings so that I could speak with him. One of the secretaries told me his attitude was like, 'Don't you know who I am? I'm the man in her life!' He would get furious when I had to go out of town for the job. And he absolutely refused to go to any of the major fund raisers that I put together for the senator. I don't know why I didn't realize what was going on with him, but I guess I didn't want to admit that even though he'd encouraged me to go to grad school, he really didn't want me to be a successful professional."

"When my friend was in dental school," Melva, the physician said, "she used to struggle to pass her tests. Right before a big test, she and her husband would always have a horrible fight. He actually started trying to sabotage her career right there in school. When she finished her residency, all the residents met as a way to formally shake hands with chiefs of staff and make some more contacts. He refused to go with her and wouldn't babysit with their two kids either. Even now, when there's some professional function she has to attend, she can never depend upon him to be there. He may promise to watch the kids, but invariably he'll get mad and then refuse."

When they attack their professions, men are attempting to minimize their wives' accomplishments and their attachment to their careers. Their goal is to subordinate their wives' interests to theirs and to create a home environment where their own lives and careers are paramount. Such men have been socialized to compete and not to support and it is difficult for them to go against that training, especially when they're feeling unsupported and cheated by their wives. Because this has been the tradition, men may feel that in order to achieve they need a woman pushing them, devoting herself to their needs. When they have instead a woman devoted to her own interests, they feel gypped.

Often, men experience an almost paranoid perception that a wife's co-workers and work friends are aiding and abetting her insubordination to her husband. Some women say they feel competition coming from their husbands toward their office mates. Lena, a 43-year-old executive in a public-relations firm, was counseled by her husband when her career and marriage began. Subsequently he dropped out of public relations to go into real estate. Lena proceeded to ascend to startling professional heights. A superstar in her business, she says her fantastic success has been misinterpreted by her husband. "He's become hideously jealous of all the associations with men I've had in my job. He began to see me as someone he couldn't control anymore. I was going away every day, out of his clutches. He projected all his self-doubts onto me. For some reason he had this image of me as a very, very loose woman doing all kinds of things. His jealously drove me bananas. I'd come home from work and he'd say, 'Who'd you have lunch with today?' or if I just mentioned I'd seen some associate he knew, he'd say, 'He's got that kind of look that turns you on, doesn't he? I've seen the way he looks at you.' I don't understand this at all. I've never had any desire for anyone other than my husband."

"George used to always say to me, 'Why do you have to go to meetings with so many men?' " Donna said with a long, heavy sigh. "I'd explain to him that I just happened to work in a male-dominated field, but I always got the feeling he suspected I was up to something."

Not all men fear infidelity from their wives, of course. And many wives suspect and accuse their husbands of fooling around with women on the job. Yet for many men, who grew up believing their wives would stay at home—away from other men—it is very difficult to cope with their wives' frequent interaction with men and women. "I felt my wife was influenced by the women on her job," said Jim, the housing specialist. "These women were inviting her out a lot. There was pressure from her co-workers to have drinks after work and go to parties. I wasn't into that. Most of the guys from her office were superficial, but they all had advanced degrees. I felt I stood equal and above them all when it came to being an intellectual heavyweight," he said in a defensive tone. "Her co-workers contributed to an attitude that made my wife feel superior to me. I resented her listening to the people on her job more than she listened to me."

Some men act out their insecurities when they go to their wives' business functions. Rather than mingle, which might help their wives' careers, these husbands stay in a corner and have minimal contact with their wives' officemates, or are hostile or condescending to them. They resent male bosses as usurpers of husbandly power. Some husbands feel that they are in direct competition with a boss for their wives' affection, loyalty, and, most of all, attention and esteem.

"In a kind of sick way, my husband was always trying to compete with my boss," Sylvia, the TV producer, told me. "Once my boss gave the whole staff a vacation at his expense. The whole time we were on the trip, my husband kept saying things like, 'This is nothing. I could do better than this.' He spent the whole time trying to belittle my boss." Men defend themselves by saying they lose patience when they see their wives put their boss's needs before theirs. "My ex-wife wanted a roommate," said John. He and his first wife, Deborah, had all the external trappings of middle-class success—a house, two cars, and two salaries. But Deborah, an accountant, was sexually aloof and demonstrated little affection during their seven-year marriage, according to John. "I felt taken for granted, unappreciated, and abused," he said. "There were times when I'd go to pick her up at work and rather than tell the boss I was waiting outside for her, Deborah would let me circle the block for an hour."

Some women admit their jobs do invade their personal time; but they say they don't know how or where to draw the line. Greg, 37, a publicist living with his wife Lisa, 34, in the suburbs of Connecticut, declares and his wife agrees that he is a supportive husband who favors her ambitions. Even he, however, was put off by the actions of his wife's former boss, a woman who owned her own company. Female bosses aren't exempt from the husband's resentment, and are often seen as being "pushy ballbreakers" with too much influence on a wife. "Lisa's old boss was unbelievable. The phone rang on Sunday night and it was the boss. She said, 'How would you like to babysit, Greg?' So I said, 'For your kids?' And she said, 'No, for your little girl.' So I handed the phone to Lisa and to make a long story short, Lisa interrupts a very intimate moment with me, gets out of bed at ten o'clock at night, and goes into her office. Then she doesn't get home until after two o'clock. I resented the whole affair. I mean, here was my wife in bed with me and her boss calls and she gets up and leaves me. Her boss could have waited. Her boss wasn't concerned at all about her family."

Greg thought his wife was unconcerned too, but Lisa said: "I think Greg resented the fact that I never knew how to say no to my boss. I obviously knew how to say no to him. When I got that call, I told him, 'Try to understand.' I was afraid if I didn't go, I'd lose my job."

Perhaps the real issue is employers who see women as far more vulnerable and therefore more exploitable than male employees. Women in general earn less and are expected to do more. Lisa's boss intimidated her by saying things like, "If you can't do the work here, maybe you're not serious about being a professional." Women say they are pleading for male support while they learn the political ropes of their jobs. They point out that they have always been expected to put up with their husbands' demanding bosses.

Women who have had children might mistake the second stage of backlash with the terrible twos their toddlers exhibit: their husbands also explode in tantrums as they act out their anger, demanding what they feel their wives won't give them: undivided attention.

"I used to call a friend and invariably, three minutes into the conversation, her husband would get on the telephone and tell her to get off, that he needed her."

"If I was the center of attention at a party or something, my husband would get very quiet," said Sylvia, the television producer. "Or other times he'd say something nasty. Or else it would be time to go."

In the second stage of backlash the tenets of feminism which underscored the initial years of the marriage come under heavy fire. The wife's retaining her own name and postponing childbirth, sharing chores, all are categorically rejected now by husbands who feel put upon and neglected. It becomes more apparent to wives during this stage just how tenuous was their husbands' commitment to the promises of an egalitarian relationship. Some women admit that they were not straightforward before their marriage on some of the very issues their husbands are now rejecting. Some confess that they assumed that their husbands shared their viewpoint and so didn't really take the time to explain what they expected from a fifty-fifty marriage or to ask their husbands' feelings about marital equality.

"I flat out refused to take James's name when we were married, something he never really said too much about," Jennifer said. "I've noticed that whenever we go to business functions and we're introduced, he gets very nervous, visibly uncomfortable. One time a woman we both had just been introduced to asked us why we didn't have the same last names. I jokingly said, 'Because he didn't want mine,' and laughed. James looked like he was going to die. I've come to believe that men feel you don't love them if you don't take their names."

If the couple has children, it is during the second stage that the husband, who has already begun sloughing off his childcare duties, makes it clear that responsibility for children is woman's work. Alice declared that her husband— though he earned far less than she—forced total responsibility for their daughter on her as a way to exert control over her. "He wants me home with the baby. He sees her as my responsibility. It didn't start out that way, but that's the way it's ending up. The other night I asked him what kind of arrangements we should make if I have to go out of town on business. He told me, 'You would have to take her with you.' Was that heavy, or what? I was stunned, just stunned."

If Alice is stunned to be swamped with childcare duties she expected to share, husbands are overwhelmed when they discover the myriad pressures taking care of children brings.

"He feels that as a result of having to take on equal responsibility for his child his career has suffered," said Kim, the clinical psychologist, about her husband of eleven years, who is a lawyer. "Before he had a child, he'd come home at seven-thirty, eat dinner, and have the energy to stay up and do some work. Now, he's taking care of a kid from five-thirty until eight-thirty, two nights a week, and that wipes him out. The biggest tension in our relationship has been around whether or not to have another child. I would like one. He flatly refuses. Indirectly, what he's telling me is, 'If you take care of this child, I'll let you have another kid.' "

During the second stage, men express even more anger at postponing having a child for the sake of a wife's career. One man I interviewed admitted he had a hidden agenda in wanting his wife to get pregnant. "Part of my reasoning was that a baby would slow her down and keep her in the house more. She'd be more available to me." Other men deny that they use children to win the upper hand in their marriages. "I think I was supportive of my wife's career," said Henry, an anesthesiologist. "We came to a mutual agreement to delay having children so that she could become more professionally established, but after seven years, I wanted an interruption. I wanted to see her at home with kids. I wanted a more traditional life. She used to say that I was just trying to prove my manhood. But that wasn't it. I just wanted some kids."

Like other men in his situation, Henry thinks of his desire to have children as natural instinct rather than chauvinism. Many men are appalled when their wives say they may never have children. They angrily reject the "babies-as-bondage" theme that some women take as a message of the women's movement. The more frustrated they become with their wives' independence, the more they desperately seek to control them through pregnancy. To be prevented from conceiving is ego deflating. They are ashamed to admit to relatives and friends that their reproductive powers are controlled by their wives. Wayne, the insurance agent, admitted that he created elaborate excuses for not having children. "I never admit to anyone that the reasons we don't have children are because of Crystal. I tell my male friends that I don't want them. I tell them that I had so many brothers and sisters when I was growing up, that I've never wanted children. That way, they think the decision is mine. If they felt Crystal was calling the shots, they might think I'm less manly."

Wayne, like a lot of his peers, considers unnatural the relentless ambition of women who are willing to sacrifice all personal goals for professional success. These men say that for many women, the equal marriage is an opportunity to be selfish and free of family responsibilities, while throwing their weight around because of "big" jobs. "I'm proud of Crystal's success," asserted Wayne. "It makes me feel that I made a good choice in my mate. In certain settings though, I'm introduced as 'the husband of' and then I feel a loss of power and position. I don't like taking a back seat. I can deal with equality, but not subordination. I feel emasculated."

Husbands claim they want to protect their wives from the stress of their jobs and from their own ambition. Crystal told me her husband believes she is a workaholic. Wayne said, "She has a strong sense of responsibility to the rest of the world. She thinks if she doesn't work hard, everything will fall apart. I believe she's getting another degree to prove to the world she can. It's causing her a lot of pain and anguish. I thought she'd give up everything else to get this degree, but the only thing she's given up has been me. She's burning out. She looks older. The world is killing her; she even gets sick more often. She never takes time for herself. She'll do things when she's tired. All of her time is scheduled."

Wayne said that in seeking to control his wife, he was also trying to bring back the exuberance he feels she's lost. "Crystal used to laugh at my jokes. She used to laugh a lot. We don't laugh together. We used to have pillow fights and go to concerts and plays. Crystal used to be a toucher, a very physical person. Now she's not. I think it's the stress of the job. I like her a lot and I want to see her happy."

Some women agree that when the job, kids, the house, and their husbands begin to call out for attention, the role of wife suffers. They admit they get more satisfaction from their work than their marriages. Their husbands know it. "She's more into her career than the marriage," said Clark, an advertising executive, tersely about his wife. "The job probably gives her more respect than I do. She needs to be in charge and I won't let her do that."

Swamped with increasing responsibilities at work, tired of fighting both corporate politics and dissatisfied husbands, many childless wives are tempted by the idea of throwing in the towel forever, or just taking a break. They fear, however, giving up the power of being a wage earner in exchange for the dependency of a nonworking wife. They worry about losing themselves in a subservient role that offers no pay, little prestige, and is rife with potential abuse.

Other women genuinely want to take time out to have families and nurture them in traditional ways. Such women see themselves exactly as Wayne sees his wife: trapped in a system that is running them ragged. Men aren't alone in feeling uncomfortable with their wives' professional aspirations and achievements. Many women, when confronted with the realities of corporate life, discover they are more suited to be full-time homemakers. Others are frustrated because they can't economically afford to take a break.

A letter to the editor of the *Philadelphia Inquirer* read:

> I returned to work almost two years ago because of necessity; I'm not working because I like to. I think it's time that an honest study be done on how employment of the wife outside the home hurts not only the husband but the rest of the family as well. Judging from what I've read, these studies, touted by all the media, appear to be conducted by the feminist, anti-family factions trying to ruin our country. I haven't read any articles that say anything praiseworthy or positive about the fulltime homemaker.

I'm not happy being forced out of my home to work. My life has been nothing but a rat race. I'm tired at the end of the workday and I'm tired of cramming my life in those few short evening hours. I'm sick of rushing to do dishes, wash and food shopping. Children don't enjoy a tired mother.

There isn't enough quality time to spend with husband or children, let alone time for myself. I don't have time to keep up relationships with friends. All this hurts me and my family.

Concerning the freedom working is supposed to give me: Working doesn't free me from anything—that time now is no longer my own. I have to work but still have to be a wife, mother and homemaker, too. Is this fulfilling? No way!

This feminist philosophy of independence, fulfillment and freedom is a fraud and I'm tired of being told I must give up my family for my career. I'm tired of hearing feminist lies of liberty and fulfillment. It's simply not true! Feminism belongs in the garbage pail and its perpetrators in Moscow.

There are pressures from every direction, but as husbands increase their hostility, women begin to feel even greater stress and the results of the second stage of backlash take their toll. When my own marriage began to unravel, I remember telling someone I felt like I was caught between the proverbial rock and a hard place. Like most working wives contending with mothering, working, and being a wife in a troubled marriage, after a while, I began to burn out: I reached a level of chronic fatigue, mental and emotional upheaval, that began to impair my ability to function. I felt crazy, depressed, and under siege. At work I was chronically behind in all my assignments. At home I tried to play catchup as a wife and mother, only to feel negligent and guilty. I was so overwhelmed, I could only manage to watch helplessly as the job and my marriage slipped away. I wanted to save them, but I was too exhausted. I was not, I fear, an extreme case.

A gradual numbing may set in as women seek to deny what is happening in their lives. Their pain and mental fatigue may precipitate sexual malaise, which further erodes their marriages. Men see their wives' refusal to have sex as another way in which they are being cheated of their manhood. If husbands recall the earlier more sexually active days of their marriage, they can't help feeling that the contrasting sexual diminishment has come about because of their wives' dedication to work. They feel their wives are becoming unsexed by their careers and resent that they are more active in their offices than they are in bed, that satisfying their partners physically seems less a priority than ironing a dress for work.

Women lose interest in sex for reasons that, of course, have nothing to do with backlash. Both men and women suffer from fears of intimacy, retreating from sex to avoid full commitment. Boring, routine sex or a traumatic sexual encounter in the past can serve to repress sexual appetite for both sexes. For some women, the exhilaration of work can leave them with little energy for sexual intimacy. Women in the past have been defined by their relationships with men but many of the current crop of professional women see their identities tied to their work. "I didn't realize how much of my sexual self had disappeared," said one head of a housing agency in Maryland. "I used to fantasize about making love and have lots of sexy random thoughts during the day. That had stopped totally. My thoughts began to be mostly about work and my next project."

Part of the sexual shutdown of professional women is due to their inability to separate their work and personal lives. Women leave their jobs tense and make love in the same state of tension. That kind of sexual encounter, sooner or later, becomes a turn-off that women want to avoid. In so doing, they submerge even more the sexual parts of their personalities.

Men have had impaired sex lives for years because of the tensions of their jobs. This may be the first generation of women to take their jobs into bed with them. And their anger. In backlash marriages, many women who can't talk about their marital unhappiness with their husbands, act out their resentment by refusing to have sex. Sexually discontent husbands point out that withdrawal from lovemaking is the way some wives wield power in their relationships. "Before my wife was elected, she seemed more willing to make love when I wanted to engage," said Ted angrily. "Now, she has no problem turning me down." "My wife and I don't have a real sex life," said another man. "We make love because she feels we should. It's scheduled and she schedules it. Once a month. Once every two months. It's up to her."

During the second stage, some wives report an inordinate demand for sex and a lot of anger when they refuse their husbands. "My husband would never force me to have sex, but if I refuse him, he'll be angry with me all the next day," the systems analyst explained.

Others say their husbands react in another extreme way and withdraw from them sexually as a way to shut them out. "I guess the way I expressed my anger was to withhold affection from my wife," confessed one executive from Virginia. "I knew when she was in the mood. My way of getting back at her for not being there for me was not being there for her in the bed."

When couples want but fail to achieve sexual fulfillment, when stress interferes with that special pleasure, their concept of their marriage obviously changes. Studies have shown that in marriages where partners reported satisfying sex lives, couples usually described their marriages as fulfilling. In that same study, those partners who reported low enjoyment of sex were more likely to label their marriages as unhappy. Having a good sex life seems to increase overall contentment among couples.

When sex is relegated to catch as catch can and women increasingly burn out, they withdraw even further from their increasingly angry, frustrated husbands. Things begin to fall apart.

I recall when they fell apart for me, when the laundry piled up and went undone, when my child's hair got a pat instead of combing, when dinner was canned and I began to be afraid, not just of subway rides, but elevators, buses, cars, and crowds on the street. It was a battle to remain sane. A close friend told me she remembers that during that period of my life my face wore the look of a drowning woman. And it is at this precise stage in backlash that many women do go under, accepting a subordinate role and giving up all hopes of equality. At the end of the second stage, many women "holler uncle" and let their husbands dominate their marriages.

Lena, the public-relations executive, seemed to be fighting to stay afloat when I interviewed her. A petite woman with razor-sharp perceptions and a finely tuned sense of humor, she was well respected in her industry and had won some of its highest awards. As a professional she radiated confidence and authority, even though she didn't always feel that way about herself. It was her homelife, she confided to me in an office the size of a posh hotel suite, that she felt unable to grasp or control. "I have a wonderful marriage, but a very tough one," she told me, a cigarette in one hand, her other hand holding the pack nervously. "If I weren't so dedicated to preserving it and I didn't have four children, it might have ended a long time ago."

When her husband left his career to go into business for himself, she became the major breadwinner in their family, a condition that hadn't changed in ten years. "His biggest problem is the money situation. I make a tremendous amount of money; he makes very little. Since he went into business, I've paid the bills. He's had to come to me for money. We fight about money and he has tremendous resentment that I have the most. In the face of my husband's rage, I began to take on total responsibility for the house and children. Everything has fallen apart as life has become more complex. It's gotten to the point where we eat pizza every night or some other kind of fast foods. It's to the point where there is always a pile of dirty clothes and dishes. We now have a cook who basically comes in and ruins good meat." There was anguish in Lena's voice and face as she continued. "I feel guilty about my kids. I'm not spending enough time with them. The quality of love and time thing only goes so far. Kids need quantity. I don't fool myself. When you're not there when the kids need stitches or there are problems at school, you feel bad. And these things have happened with me. A lot. Two of my children are clearly having problems.

"Sure I've considered quitting my job. There were times seeing moms with their kids I yearned to be home. But I have to admit that type of yearning always came when the job wasn't satisfactory. And besides, our financial situation won't support my leaving. I come from a fiercely ambitious family. I'm cut out to have a career.

"I get the most satisfaction, the feeling that I'm doing it right, from my profession. It's constant. I have a reputation in this industry. I'm one of the few female stars around. Yet, at the same time, I have doubts about even my career. I have to leave my office at five o'clock every day and there are days I need to stay longer. I feel absolutely negligent about everything. I had a mini breakdown not too long ago. It happened right after my husband had a complete mental breakdown. I sort of luxuriated in falling apart. I feel that I've failed, failed as a mother, a wife, and a professional. Sometimes I want to run away from everything. I realize that's not rational, but that's the way I feel sometimes."

I could identify with everything Lena told me. And with the anguish of being trapped between two worlds. My final look at her through closing elevator doors revealed cold, naked desperation. A pretty face full of pain. The drowning look, as my friend called it.

7

Stage III: All Out War

I was surprised when the phone rang for me at my cousin's apartment in New York, only moments after I'd arrived. When the woman gave her name, I recognized it. I had intended to call Alice at the suggestion of a woman I'd interviewed in Philadelphia. Alice wanted to be interviewed, she explained on the telephone. She wanted to sort out what was happening in her marriage and from what her friend had told her, she believed I could help. I was talking about her life. Could I meet her for drinks in thirty minutes?

We met in the lobby of the mammoth building where she worked. I was expecting a stylish, sophisticated woman to match the mature, businesslike voice on the phone, but Alice emerged from the elevator looking disheveled, almost waif-like, in a skirt and sweater, her hair messy in the way hair gets messy when fingers run nervously through it all day long. She certainly wasn't dressed for success, yet at 29, she commanded nearly $40,000 annually and had a position of authority.

Her life was stressful enough already, she told me while we sat at the quiet, elegant Japanese restaurant we chose because there was little background noise to interfere with the taping. Her husband was trying to control her, she claimed, trying to force her into a subservient, dependent mode that was in direct contrast to the way they'd agreed their marriage would be. Ever since her daughter had been born more than a year ago, he'd stopped helping with house-work, was criticizing her viciously and becoming angrier and angrier when she refused to knuckle under. She had tried to be patient, she claimed. She'd tried to build up his ego, to be supportive, to go along with some of his demands, but he was getting to be even more of a tyrant. She'd had enough she said, in a voice that was strong and determined. And she was beginning to tell him so. She was an independent woman, she told me. Her mother had been divorced and had owned her own home, gone to work, and raised three children who'd all turned out okay. "I always knew that women could make it on their own. I was never one of those women who had to have a man," she said, sipping her wine.

Last week she'd come home to find the dishes her husband had used, sitting in the sink on top of others he'd left there. Her "on strike" tactic was getting nowhere. He'd left dirty dishes in the sink for three days running. Finally, she exploded, marching into their bedroom where he lay across the bed watching television. She said she'd screamed so loudly that she surprised herself. "Forget this," she'd yelled. "I'm not coming home and doing every damn thing in this house. I'm not trying to be superwoman and if you're trying to make me one, forget it. If you're supposed to be my husband then you take part of the weight."

"That's exactly what I told him," Alice said, nodding her head, sipping her wine. "How can a healthy man leave dirty plates for three days? How can a man try to control his wife through their child? I just don't understand it," she said, then added softly, "Some women may feel that they have to do everything to keep a man, but I don't. The hell with that."

Stage III backlash is women striking back. Those who haven't thrown in the towel fight to avoid being dominated by husbands and to maintain equality in their marriages. Stage III is ushered in when women go from blithely thinking of themselves as equal, to feeling harassed, to attempting to be superwomen, to considering themselves the martyred victims of burnout. They begin to acknowledge their rage and they turn it on their husbands.

Not all women are able to do that. Because of the way they've been socialized, many, whether they can acknowledge it or not, are too intimidated by male anger to even put up a defense against it, let alone launch an offensive battle to get the kind of marriage that works for them. But women who are more empowered and resilient learn to fight fire with fire. In Stage III women and men shout their deepest resentments, each hoping to force the other person to see their viewpoint, or at least to punish for the hurt they received. They express their anger verbally, sexually, and even physically. Drugs or alcohol may be abused.

Men, in an effort to maintain their sense of masculinity, act in ways that their wives deem irrational, while women defiantly move even further away from traditionalism. Backlash has forced many women into a position where they are no longer able to blend the traditional and professional parts of their personalities. They feel pushed into abandoning the homemaker role by the very person who claimed to value it most. Women begin to submerge themselves in their jobs, not necessarily because their careers are so fulfilling, but because after endlessly battling with husbands at home, the office seems less hostile than their homes. As backlash escalates, more and more women reject the role of wife.

"I'm not one of those career-hungry women," said Karen, a high-ranking executive in a large company. "To me what I do is a job; it helps me earn the money to do what I want to do. I didn't claw my way to the top, but I'm good and I've been fortunate."

She describes her marriage as tense. She and her husband, Dennis, are in the same field, but he isn't nearly as successful. She is by far the superior earner and her $60,000-plus salary greatly exceeds her husband's wages as an independent consultant. She says that her husband is intimidated by her earning power, her professional reputation, and her credentials. "He has the feeling he's got to be smarter than I am. He feels that I don't respect his talents. If I were less an 'important' person it would be easier for him. He wants to own my abilities and have them work for him. When he asks me to help him to proofread something of his, he wants it done immediately. If I ask him to wait, he gets angry and walks away."

Karen says that the tension in her relationship with Dennis has caused both of them to explode in anger. If she once held her tongue, she no longer does. Compared to her marriage, her job is an oasis of calm. "I think he feels that I'm more conscientious about my job than our relationship. Sometimes that's true. Sometimes I hide in my job, because I can do it without conflict as opposed to dealing with a very difficult relationship."

"I've begun to feel that business gives me more strokes," said Joan, 34, an entrepreneur who says her successful company cost her her marriage to a man she feels was too insecure to allow her to achieve. "Business is challenging. My husband was discouraging. Business gives me rewards; my husband belittled me."

A certain number of the women interviewed admitted that their professional lives aren't ideal. They are still conflicted about leaving young children with sitters and giving short shrift to their homemaking responsibilities in order to work outside the home. They fear becoming less feminine. Like their men, philosophically, they agree with the tenets of the women's movement—that women need to have the equal right to be wage earners—but, psychologically, they are conflicted about melding their careers and their marriages. Most were brought up to be homemakers who are financially supported by their husbands and yet their jobs represent something they have come to value highly: economic independence. While many women may be caught between wanting to be taken care of and wanting independence, most recognize and enjoy the benefits of having their own money. When their independence is placed in jeopardy by husbands who fear their loss of control, many, even ambivalent women, realize that they have options in their marriages only because they are wage earners. Having money, even if it isn't enough money, means they don't have to accept their husbands' negative behavior. The bottom line is, they aren't totally dependent on their husbands. Many women can make it on their own.

I could feel the tension in Ted and Flo's house as I sat unpacking my tape recorder. The snatches of words floating around me seemed propelled by anger. Ted and Flo were spitefully jabbing at each other, trying to wound. They had been married for seven years and had two children, a boy of five and a daughter who was three. Flo held public office in the city where she and her husband lived. She told me that she'd campaigned hard and won against a popular opponent. Her work, she said, her blue eyes brimming with enthusiasm, was challenging and at times, all consuming. She was highly visible and constantly in demand to speak and to serve her constituency in one way or another. It was difficult to balance her lofty public image with the realities of being a wife and mother of two children.

"Entrepreneur," Ted said when I asked his occupation. He said the word loudly and resolutely, almost as if challenging me to dispute him. Ted was an engineer by profession, but informed me that he was seeking financial backing for an invention that he felt would lead to great wealth in the future.

It was obvious that children lived in the couple's spacious home. Every room had some remnants of toys or clothing strewn carelessly about. There were dishes in the kitchen, toys on the living-room floor, and crumbs on several of the tables in the house. The two children's rooms looked as though a cyclone had ripped through them and then turned around and came back; Flo and Ted's bedroom was only slightly less damaged looking.

Flo had banished her daughter and son to the basement playroom in order to give us enough peace to conduct an interview. Still, I could hear her children's screams of delight and anger as I asked my questions; the thuds of their feet on the hard floor made constant background noise. Every so often, the little girl would make an appearance at the top of the stairs, look anxiously around, and make a beeline for Flo. I'd have to press the pause button on my tape recorder, while her mother listened to the child's request. If Ted was talking he'd raise his voice in an effort to continue, unless his daughter's ruckus was impossible to shut out. Then he would give his wife an annoyed look that seemed to say, "Can't you keep that child quiet?" Several times Flo got up to give her daughter a cookie or some toy to quiet her down a bit. The last time the daughter interrupted us, Flo attended to her with a visible show of impatience, a look of frustration crossing her face as her eyes met Ted's; he sat on the sofa, smoking and somewhat belligerently watching his wife and child.

In the years since the children had been born, Flo had gradually taken over the majority of the childcare and house-work. This, combined with her work in politics, made her feel stretched beyond her limits. The division of labor was a sore spot in their household, I realized, as the couple's voices rose and they cut across each other with angry snarls. Ted, she said, had little comprehension of the amount of work she had to do to maintain their home. Ted argued that his male-oriented duties were even more stressful than his wife's.

That Ted was so open about the delineation of male and female responsibilities surprised me. He told me that his views on appropriate roles for men and women came from his upbringing. His father was a carpenter. His mother "raised the kids and took care of the house," but also did hairdressing in her home for private customers. Ted said that as a young boy he was taught how to sew, cook, and do dishes as well as carpentry. Those early lessons had stuck, he said. He still hemmed his own pants and sewed on all the buttons for everyone in the house. And, he said with deep and obvious pride, he could repair anything that went wrong in his house, from plumbing to electricity. Although he had always favored traditional marriages, when he met Flo and realized she wanted a career, he had pitched in . . . for a while. Now he was back to square one. He wanted a traditional marriage.

Flo's upbringing had been middle class. Her father was a doctor and her mother a housewife until Flo was in high school, when she returned to teaching. Both Flo's parents had wanted her to achieve, even to overachieve. She was told that she should be independent and able to take care of herself. Her parents also stressed domestic chores, both for her and her two older sisters. Even as a child, though, Flo recognized that she didn't really enjoy homemaking and determined early on that when she grew up she would pay someone to do those things for her. "Ted calls that buying my way out," she told me. Then she shrugged. A hostile look crossed Ted's face. Listening to them discuss, then argue about their problems, I felt that I was coming in at the beginning of the end of a very long battle.

"Ted and I have totally different perspectives about how our household is going," said Flo. "From my perspective there are an incredible number of day-to-day chores to get the children together. The kids have to eat. I have to have dinner every day. Someone has to prepare those meals and it's always me," she said wearily, avoiding her husband's eyes.

"Always? Or most of the time?" Ted asked her.

Flo faced her husband and said succinctly, "Ninety-five percent of the time it's me. From September to June I believe that it's always me. Of course," she added quickly, "Ted does clear the gutters and shovel the snow out and cut the grass, but I wouldn't do that at all. We used to have a cleaning lady, but I'm the only one working now. We can't afford her anymore."

He seemed to feel betrayed when Flo mentioned his unemployment. I felt that he was covering his hurt pride when he launched into a diatribe about the important work he did around his house.

"Well, I agree Flo has the responsibility for the children and the house," he said testily. "However, one hundred percent of the time it's my responsibility to take care of the more important functions around the house that Flo can't do. Like when the grass needs to be cut, Flo doesn't know how to put gas in the mower or start it up. In the winter when it snows, it's my job one hundred percent of the time to shovel the pavement and clear off the cars. I paint the walls. I make plumbing repairs. I do housework as well. I'm the only one who can efficiently clean up the kitchen," he said, his voice rising and quivering with sarcasm and anger. "And, I don't get any help for my work. I don't ask for any. I'd like to see that philosophy reciprocated when she's doing something for the kids."

Flo's voice rose to meet her husband's, decibel for decibel. "The point is, I have a challenging job. At the end of the day, I can't think. Then I have to pick up two kids, come home, and cook dinner. I give the kids their baths, read them a story, fix their lunches. The next day, I get them dressed, fix breakfast, and take them to school. I have a much more stressful day than you," she said, her mouth tight and tense.

"Since you've been elected, your ego has expanded so much that you feel you don't have to give me what I need," he said directly to Flo. Then he turned to me. "Before she was elected I could get a decent meal if I wanted one," he said, emphasizing the word *decent*. "Now when I ask for dinner I get what I get, usually something half-assed that she's thrown together. I'm also unhappy about what her professional life has meant for Flo's physical upkeep of her body," he continued louder. "You're fatter. You're not exercising, just sitting in those hallowed halls," he said sarcastically. "Then you come home and try to throw your weight around here. Being a council person is number one with you," Ted said bitterly. "The family is number two. You'll give one hundred fifty percent in the city council and only fifty percent at home. I'd rather see you perform as a wife."

"You get benefits from my position," Flo retorted. "He's quick to say, this is my wife, the councilwoman. He mentions it more than I do."

Ted paused for a moment as if caught off guard. Then he said quietly, "I'm proud of you."

I could see what was going on with this couple in a way I hadn't been able to see what was happening five years earlier when I stood outside Gloria and Ben's door and overheard the loud angry frustration that eventually ended their marriage. Flo and Ted seemed just as hostile toward each other as my friend and her husband had been. They were in touch with their rage and out of touch with each other. It seemed clear to me that *each* of them was trying to use the part of an egalitarian relationship that was convenient and was fighting to discard the other parts. Ted wanted Flo's economic support while his fledgling enterprise took off, but he also wanted an old-fashioned wife to take care of the house and children. Ted didn't want to relinquish what, for him, defined his masculinity: women took care of children and the house, not men. Flo wanted a handyman who was willing to share the responsibilities of children and the house-work, but she balked when Ted expected her to carry the entire financial load. And despite the fact that she wanted an egalitarian marriage, Flo wasn't prepared to sacrifice her femininity—her right to be taken care of—to that end. Un-willing to bend, Ted and Flo were actually breaking the bonds that had once held them together.

I didn't stay around Flo and Ted long enough to see any indications that they expressed their anger beyond hot words. There are more subtle indicators that the third stage is under way, a large grab bag of mean tricks that spouses play on one another: women burn dinners they didn't want to cook in the first place; men disappear when they promised to babysit for their children while their wives do something career-related; both are chronically late for each other; both stay out of the house in order to anger the partner; both punish each other with silence. Once again sex is used as an instrument of anger and punishment by men and women.

"As our marriage declined and my business made more and more money, sex became very slam, bam, thank you ma'am," said Joan. "There wasn't an attempt to satisfy me.

The sexual act was an extension of what he was feeling. He felt diminished by my success. He wasn't confident as a human being."

"My husband and I had a lot of angry sex," said Sylvia, the award-winning producer. "He'd get mad about something, then we'd make up and have sex." She says that because of the constant tension surrounding the relationship, the couple's love life was never really relaxed.

While angry sex, insensitive sex, and the withholding of sex are overtly threatening to a marriage and dramatically escalate hostilities, there is a more subtle kind of sexual shutdown that is even more devastating. Sometimes, because they are so angry, men begin to experience what they feared as a by-product of their wives' independence: sexual impotence.

At 45, Angela, a reporter for a major newspaper, was slightly older than most of the women I'd interviewed. Her balanced sensibilities placed her with an elite group of women who, in embracing their professional selves, hadn't abandoned their femininity. We met at her paper, after she'd written a story that would appear on the front page of the next edition. The intensity of her job rendered her unable to do many of the more domestic things that she liked but no longer had time for. She adjusted and reveled in the intellectual satisfaction that her job gave her. She would have felt complete except, she told me, her husband had resented the fact that her job took her away from his control. She and her husband had been separated for several years. Only recently had a matured hindsight enabled her to judge why their relationship had failed. "He would have been content if I'd never read a book, never encountered life in any way," said Angela sadly. "He's a classic passive/aggressive. I grew and changed and I thought he did too, but he hadn't. His backlash was so incredibly subtle. He found ways to beat up on me and it took me a very long time to figure it out. For example, when I asked him to do things around the house, he never protested. He simply would forget to put in the load of clothes or mop the floor or cook the dinner. He couldn't verbalize that he was feeling threatened by my independence. Once I asked him if he wanted me home more and he gave me this ambivalent spate: yes, he wanted me around more and also he was very proud of my accomplishments. He didn't know how to confront me with the anger that was building up inside him because I was gone so much and so successful, so he'd yell at our oldest daughter who looks just like me. After a while, I saw through that. I'd say, 'Look, leave her alone. What's your issue with me?' He gave the appearance of being proud and supportive of me. If someone said, 'Oh, I really like your wife's articles,' he'd say, 'Yes, she is really doing a good job.' Then he'd come and say to me, 'Four people asked me about your reporting yesterday. I really get tired of answering questions about your job.' When we finally had to deal with the marriage, he said he felt that I didn't need him. Maybe that's true. I didn't need him financially or emotionally. The ways I needed him, he was unable to give."

Angela believed her husband's childhood was responsible

for the way he related to her. "His mother was a classic controlling housewife. She ruled, but in a very subtle way. If things didn't go the way she wanted them to go, she'd get sick. And I mean she wouldn't get up from her bed. Then, from that sickbed, she would dictate and her husband would be forced to do everything she wanted him to do. I think my husband had a lot of bottled-up rage toward his mother and he passed that rage on to me."

The anger finally manifested in their bed. "He developed a classic case of impotence," Angela said in a quiet voice. "We'd never had a passionate sex life, but there had never been a problem. The impotence occurred after I got more visible at the paper. As I seemed to need him less, his withdrawal from me became sexual. I think his anger was so deep and complete that he got me in a way that was deep for me.

"I felt a lot of anguish about what was happening. I was, at first, loving and sympathetic. Then I went through the stage where I said we had to talk. Next I went through the stage where I felt it was me, that I was undesirable. I felt I was a great failure."

What annoyed Angela was that her husband was anxious to maintain the fiction of a happy marriage in public, despite their private torture. "He couldn't have been more affectionate when people were around. I finally said to him, 'Look, we have to face the fact that your body is telling you something that your mind won't deal with and you have to listen to your body because it's more honest than you are.' " Angela said the end result of her husband's impotence was something she was grateful for: their separation. "I'm glad his body dumped out on us. We might have gone on way too long."

The fifty-fifty marriage doesn't threaten women in exactly that way. Women plead for understanding when they are tired or not in the mood to make love, but their emotional lack of desire doesn't preclude their ability to engage in sex, nor does it diminish their womanliness. Husbands who are persistent enough and selfish enough can satisfy themselves physically, if not emotionally, whether their wives want to make love or are just "going along with the program." Husbands may think of their wives as cold or even frigid, but rarely as nonfunctional. Women don't fear becoming impotent. Indeed, society is far more accepting of a woman's lack of sexual desire (Not tonight, honey, I have a headache) than they are of a man's lack of sexual prowess. When men see women gaining in independence, they see themselves losing in manliness. If their fears of lessened potency are manifested physically, the sad truth is that eventually many women do withdraw from their husbands. To cover the loss of control they feel and in an attempt to regain it, some men may react violently during the third stage of backlash.

"My husband started abusing me verbally at first," recalled Beatrice, the college professor. "He accused me of running around. He'd ask me things like 'Whose phone number is this?' 'Whose toothbrush is this in the bathroom?' Then he started to drink a lot. He would get really loud and vile. He'd degrade me. He told me I was nothing. Then finally, he became physically abusive."

Melva recalled that her dentist friend received physical abuse from her husband. "She couldn't attend her dental school graduation because he had beaten her," Melva declared.

Although Joan, the business owner, was never beaten, she says her husband was violent to their children. "He maintained a violent tone. I think that he spanked our children abusively," she said.

I remember the defensive, ashamed expression on Jim's face when he admitted he had succumbed to violence with his wife. The federal executive angrily told me that his wife's idea of an equal relationship was only a ploy to enable her to have less responsibility. "We were both working, but she said that she had a problem paying half the rent. She wanted a seventy-thirty situation, saying that she should pay less because she cooked. I was totally upset with that. I felt that she was reneging."

Jim felt even more threatened when it appeared his wife was trying to cut him out of her life completely. "She was having problems with her car and on one particular Saturday she said that she was going to look for a new car. I asked to go. She said no. She went with her mother and sister. She came home later and said, 'I got a new car.' I said, 'You got a what? Where did you get the money?' I saw the bill of sale. It said that she'd paid cash. She told me, 'It's none of your business.' I learned later that she got the money from her mother.

"Not long after that, I had planned a birthday surprise

for my wife one weekday evening. It got late and she hadn't called me. Finally, she called and said she was at the house of a co-worker. I asked her to come home. She said that she wasn't ready to and hung up." When she did come home, Jim admits that he became enraged and physically abused her. "I kicked her in the rear end."

Violence is an extreme form of the kind of "macho stance" men take when they feel their masculinity is in jeopardy. Men who are threatened by their wives' ability to compete and in some cases surpass them at the moneymaking game, often try to flex their muscles in other ways. Husbands may begin to stay out all night as a show of male potency. Others, whose wives earn significantly more money, quit their jobs and strike out on their own, posturing as entrepreneurs who can earn more than their successful wives. These businesses usually appear suddenly and seem poorly planned to the wives. They are always "his" business, although a great deal of the time the men will demand that their wives help them and invest the family money—much of which the wife has earned. For many husbands, these enterprises represent the means by which they can rescue their manhood. Wives say the businesses take on a fantasy quality: the men will make a million dollars, regain the control of their wives and thus their masculinity. Unfortunately, what often results is an even greater loss of ego. When these businesses do not get off the ground, wives are forced to become the sole supporters of their family, giving men even less control and rankling women.

Sue, the community-center director from Chicago, described her husband's reaction when her salary began to approach his earnings as a physicist for a major corporation. "Without consulting me, he quit his job and opened his own consulting firm. The whole venture was poorly planned and ill-timed. His business failed miserably. He just wasn't the entrepreneurial type."

Beatrice, the college professor, said her husband quit his job at the spur of the moment too. "I think he wanted to succeed in business in order to overshadow me. He told me, 'I want you to be proud of me.' When he quit his job, he didn't talk it over with me. He wanted a furniture business. I suggested that he hire someone to work in the store and we could work it on weekends. He insisted on going into it full time. It was a shock because we hadn't financially prepared for it. We borrowed from my mother, the bank, and he found an established businessman for a partner. They bought a building together.

"The business didn't go well at all. All the money they made, which wasn't much, went back into the business. Our marriage really started to slide. He never told me anything about the business. We had borrowed this money together, but he didn't want me to even come to the store. It was *his* business."

Carol, a highly paid executive, said, "One week my husband told me, 'I really would like to go out on my own. I'm not happy.' The next week he quit his job." She had instantly become the sole breadwinner and admitted she resented her husband's capricious move. She doesn't believe in his dream of independence and doesn't think he does either. Like many women, Carol feels exploited and is losing respect for her husband because he isn't earning money. "I think he's using this time to take a break," she said thoughtfully. "He's doing some recreational things. I'm feeling resentful. I have to do a lot of sacrificing for him. I feel that by this time, I should be cruising instead of still struggling."

The living room heated up even more in Flo and Ted's home when their dialogue turned to Ted's lack of employment. Hot words were exchanged and the two went around and around for a spell, Flo accusing, Ted defending. They shouted and cut each other off until we were all tired. Finally, Ted turned to me and said, "You talk about husband backlash, well, what about wife backlash? I receive a lot of criticism from Flo for not working a job and for trying to make my dreams come true. If I were supporting her and she wasn't working, wouldn't that be okay?" he asked, looking toward his wife. She didn't answer.

Ted and Flo seemed to call a truce as they walked me to the door, but I could still feel the anger swirling around me. Before I left, Flo asked me what I thought about them. What were their chances? I hedged, of course, not wanting to play marriage counselor. What were their chances? I asked myself later. Where would all of their hot words and anger take them? Would Ted begin to look elsewhere for validation and confirmation of his masculinity? Would Flo search for comfort in the arms of a more supportive man? Or would the need for emotional self-preservation pull the couple even further apart, pull them all the way to Stage IV?

8

Stage IV: Terminal Affairs

T he voice on the telephone was familiar, even though I hadn't heard it in years. Richard, an old friend from college was in town and wanted to get together. I'd been separated for nearly two years and was barely managing in my roles of single mother and working woman. A relaxing evening with an old friend in a restaurant I couldn't afford sounded like heaven. I accepted his invitation gratefully.

Even in the dim light of the restaurant, Richard, in his dark, three-piece business suit, looked prosperous. "You must be doing all right," I kidded him. He returned the compliment, effusively telling me my dress was "fabulous," my hair "great." Something in his tone put me on guard. I was looking good he told me, over and over and over.

After a glass of wine and lots of chitchat, we began catching up on our lives. It was a strangely stilted conversation. Richard asked me questions about my child and my work, but I could tell he wasn't really interested in any of my responses. We managed to banter back and forth about our aspirations, but all the while I sensed that something was disturbing him, that he wanted me to stop talking and listen to him.

I don't know how we started the conversations about our marriages, but when we did, the floodgates lifted and Richard's charming demeanor changed. He and his wife weren't getting along, he told me. She was "into this career thing, you know," he said, looking beyond me, a dark expression on his face. His voice was bitter. He felt cheated, he told me. He wanted children and she wasn't ready. He wanted companionship and she wasn't available. All of her energies went into her work; she wanted to be a big success, he said, spitting out the word *success*.

Seeing the startled look on my face, he quickly explained that he liked ambitious women. Hell, he had to admire anyone who could stay up all night long to get a project out. He'd helped her to become the big deal she was, Richard declared. She didn't want to cook, okay, he'd gone along with that. Most of the time they ate out or brought home fast food. It did bother him, though, that she couldn't ever find the time to cook his favorite food, spaghetti and meat balls, even once in a while. She didn't have to clean. They had a woman come in to do it, although he didn't see why they needed one, with just the two of them. They'd kept the maid even when his wife wasn't working for a short spell. "And she never stopped buying silk blouses during that time, either," he said so hotly his words sounded like tiny explosions. I could smell his anger.

Needing to expend some energy, I laughed nervously. Richard gave me a look of profound gratitude and reached for my hand. The gesture said, "You understand, don't you? You're not like her." I laughed again, and it had a cracking sound in it.

Richard held on to my hand even when my palms began to get moist, and began telling me about his successful business. He'd quit his job as an administrator for a transportation company and was operating a "cabulance" service, transporting handicapped and infirm people to hospitals and therapy centers. Although his business had been in operation less than a year, he envisioned rapid growth. He'd just been marking time at his old job, he said with obvious pride. He was the kind of man who had to make a mark in the world, not waste his life scrounging for pennies as somebody else's employee. His wife couldn't appreciate his ambition and drive. She was "so busy doing her own thing she doesn't want to help me do our thing."

There was something so pitiful and disturbing in Richard's eyes when he described his big success to me, steadily increasing the pressure of his hand. Think I'm important, his eyes said. Believe in me. He wanted validation from an old friend; but more important, he seemed to desperately need approval from a potential lover. Richard looked deeply into my eyes and I could feel him trying to muster up some charm, some charisma. Oh, God, I thought, here it comes.

He squeezed my hand so vigorously he almost spilled the wine in front of us. He and his wife were having sexual problems. "She, uh, doesn't seem able to be really fulfilled. Isn't really all that interested, actually." I began to cough. He'd started seeing other women, he told me, his voice taking on a confessional tone. He wasn't the type, though, to go from bed to bed, especially with all the diseases that were out there today. He was thinking about leaving his wife. He was ready for a real relationship. I felt the pressure of his hand bearing down hard on mine.

"Your basic 'my wife doesn't understand me' bullshit," my girlfriend confirmed when I described the night to her a few days later.

"Very basic," I said ruefully. I wanted to trivialize the encounter, to strip Richard of his individual pathos and lump him with the rest of the world's womanizers. I couldn't do that. I felt sorry for him. Richard had seemed so unlike the self-confident man I'd known years before. The old Richard had dazzled and charmed everyone with his exuberant gusto and man-about-town *joi de vivre*. The man I'd had dinner with seemed to be begging for acceptance, eager to be affirmed as desirable and worthwhile. That man seemed to need an affair to validate his manhood.

When I declined Richard's advances that night, I turned down the opportunity to play a pivotal role in the fourth stage of his marital backlash. I was giving up the chance to become the final catalyst that might possibly spark the dissolution of his marriage, or force both him and his wife to come to new terms.

In a backlash marriage, both men and women may begin extramarital relationships. At this stage of backlash, however, it is the husbands who react specifically to their insecurity about their wives' success by looking outside the relationship for emotional and sexual affirmation. Unfortunately, for many men, adultery is one of the few outlets for nursing hurt feelings and wounded pride. Because of the way men have been socialized, most male friendships or even kin relationships are devoid of emotional sharing. A few men may turn to sports or other outside interests. One self-employed lawyer said his troubled marriage has propelled him into workaholism. He is pragmatic about why he doesn't engage in an affair. "People don't want to give their business to men who aren't faithful, especially women."

Frequently, however, when males feel abandoned by their wives, they turn to another woman with the feeling: If my wife won't give me what I need, I can get it elsewhere. In addition, part of the attraction of an affair is that it places the male in a familiar and secure dating ritual. Men can feel more dominant, more in control, especially, when they are picking up the tab. Extramarital relationships are also a safe-guard against loneliness. People can dash from one relationship into another without ever experiencing emotional deprivation or fully owning up to their part in the dissolution of their marriages. It is hard to turn down pleasure when their own marriages present them with so much pain. "Other women look up to me and give me a lot of attention," said Derrick, a salesman, summing up what many men receive from the "other woman."

Many of the men I spoke with declare they aren't habitual philanderers, indeed, some swear they've never had an affair. Nevertheless, they all agree that the conditions in which an affair takes place have at one point been present in their marriages. What entices men away from their wives, they say, isn't necessarily a pretty face or a sexy figure. Men say they gravitate toward women who affirm their masculinity and tend to move away from women who negate or ignore it. The kind of women married men choose to have affairs with often are a better illustration of their needs than what they've been able to communicate to their spouses.

Yet, even in a world where the double standard favors male infidelity and tacitly supports it, many men agonize about their decision to commit adultery. They strive to make their marriages work. After seven years of marriage, Nick, a manager for an automobile leasing agency, felt ignored and abused by his businesswoman wife. He yearned for children but his spouse put off childbearing while she climbed the corporate ladder. Nick claims his needs for support and appreciation went unmet in his marriage. Feeling unappreciated and unmanly, he sought solace from another woman.

"I'm basically a pretty straight guy. I wasn't in the habit of running around on my wife. In the beginning I upheld my marriage vows and I would have continued had things been right between us. But I saw my wife as a woman who really didn't need me. We reached such an impasse I could see that nothing was going to work out. I began feeling more and more cheated. Then I met a woman who seemed to care about me. Even though I was drawn to her, I tried to save my marriage. My relationship with the other woman didn't become physical for more than a year after I met her."

Unlike his wife, his lover didn't have a college degree. Nick admits that her devotion to him and her dependency struck a harmonious chord with him. "I grew up in a traditional home. Maybe if my mother had been a lawyer or an accountant, I'd have been prepared to cope with all the problems that occur when two people work. I think a career woman is a bigamist; she's married to the job and her husband. Something has to give." In Nick's case, it was his first marriage. He is now married to his former lover, who stays home with their children. He says he is happier. "There are times when I miss the intellectual stimulation I had with my first wife, but I've gained a real family life."

Some husbands use the fact that their professional wives are busy as a rationalization for having affairs—when that was their intention regardless of their marital circumstances. Men who are seeking avenues to relieve themselves of moral restrictions may create and set up situations to soothe their guilt. They may goad their wives into behavior that allows them to escalate backlash and escape into extramarital affairs.

Like Nick, many men married to successful women choose to have affairs with women who are willing to be subordinate to them. All women aren't committed to equality between the sexes. In an era when the stigma of an unmarried woman having sex and the fear of pregnancy have been removed, married men can find women willing to have affairs, particularly if there is any possibility that such a liaison may lead to marriage.

"In retrospect, I see where I neglected my husband," said Aurelia. "Going to school awakened so much in me that had been dormant. I was in love with the whole experience of growing. I shut him out. I concentrated on me and my development, me and my learning, me and my dreams." Unable to penetrate the barrier that Aurelia admits she erected, her husband found another woman with whom he could share his dreams and be the more dominant person in the relationship.

"He had an affair with a more traditional woman, a woman who had a job and not a career. She could be there totally for him at the end of the day. She could cook and keep house and do everything he wanted." Her husband left Aurelia for his lover and later married her. "If we could have talked things out instead of acting out, maybe we would still be together," she said.

Interestingly, not all men choose to have affairs with subordinate women. Some deliberately select women who might be peers of their wives. In choosing a successful woman with whom to have an affair, they are in effect saying to their wives: "I can have a woman as powerful as you who will also submit to me. I can replace you."

"I'm a workaholic," declared Grace, a buyer for a department store in Indiana. She admits she neglected her husband: "I began working a great deal and doing a lot of traveling for my job. My husband resented the fact that I wasn't there. He wanted a companion. He'd get really angry and say to me, 'You're spending all week long getting ready for this trip! I haven't seen you.' Then he'd withdraw and not communicate at all. He got involved with yoga and I wasn't interested at all. He met a woman who was, or at least professed to be. The thing was, this woman was even more of a professional than I was and she had to be just as busy. She owned a store. But I guess she gave him the undivided attention he needed when they were together."

Women are well aware that sometimes it is the waning sexual activity in a marriage that leads to faithlessness. "George reacted when I strayed from my job, which was to be his companion," said Donna succinctly. "I'd always been very sexually active, but after I started working, I was exhausted a lot. Sometimes I just didn't feel like making love. When I made excuses, he told me, 'If you don't want to do this, I'll find someone who does.' He would get totally enraged. He was true to his word, too. He had an affair with a very passive woman." Donna said the affair was fairly obvious. "People don't stay out all night long at meetings. Then, of course, there were times she called."

Donna said George's affair precipitated their breakup. He

married the other woman. Two years later, she is still stunned by the outcome. "The thing is, I can't imagine him with a subservient woman. I didn't know that's what he wanted. But everybody says his wife just sort of hangs on to his every word and that he really seems to like that. I heard she didn't work during the beginning of their marriage and that in a year or so, she's had several 'little' jobs. He's her career."

Most wives don't condone male infidelity, even if they feel they bear some responsibility for it. They are even less empathetic with men who cope with female success by becoming constant philanderers. "I found out after my husband and I split up that he was having a series of affairs with women who reported to him," said Sylvia, the television producer. "It was very clear to me why he was running around with all these underlings. He could dominate them. He must have been far more insecure than I ever imagined. Somebody told me he once went to a party with one woman and another woman he was running around with was there and they began arguing about who was going to be with him."

When a man has a string of extramarital affairs, backlash isn't the only reason. The chronic philanderer has basic insecurity problems that marriage to a successful woman only exacerbates. Often their affairs take on a harshly punitive tone as men flaunt obvious signs of infidelity before their wives. Such men want to be caught. They are striking out to hurt.

The dentist's husband was a womanizer who didn't bother

to cover his tracks, Melva told me. "He gets back at his wife for being successful by having women and being very, very obvious about it. The other women he deals with are all subservient to him. He lets the evidence of his infidelity, if not the woman herself, lie all around their house. My friend has told me she's found lipsticks, combs, even a pair of panties. It hurts her. Women have called her house. It's hard to understand what motivates him, other than a very obvious desire to be cruel to her."

Sylvia said it wasn't until after her divorce that she realized how much her husband needed to hurt her. "After we separated, he called me to let me know he was with someone new. He said, 'I'm with a real woman now, not a woman trying to be a man.' "

The serious affair has an even more devastating effect on the marriage than multiple extramarital relationships. Most men, both "playboys" and steadier types, don't intend to fall in love with the "other woman" and leave their marriages. Men who engage in long affairs, however, are more likely to do just that. The longer the relationship continues, the greater the chances the male may get deeply involved—financially and emotionally. As time goes by, these men pay less attention to their marriages and more to their lovers. They begin scheduling time so they can be with the other woman. Eventually, they look for ways to get out of the marriage.

Male infidelity feeds upon female insecurity. It is a cultural expectation that women, far more than men, have mates.

Independent women are just as likely as traditional women to feel vulnerable and fearful of loneliness and life without a man. Even though they earn their own salary, such women believe they can't make it in the world without a man by their side. They tend to turn a blind eye to their man's unfaithfulness. "My friend stays because she's afraid to be by herself," said Melva. "It never occurs to her, this woman who put herself through dental school while raising kids, that she can function without a man."

Men often take advantage of that kind of fear and use it to control their wives. "I could be with a lot of different women. I don't have to stay with you," one chronic philanderer told his wife. Some women, motivated by their insecurity, their financial liability, and a desire to ease marital tensions, strike a bargain: she can be ambitious and achieving and he can have other women. "I've seen a number of relationships that are basically just arrangements," said Dan, 36, an economist. "She may make a lot more money than he does and he doesn't feel great about that. So, he runs around. And she doesn't really care about him emotionally or sexually, but she doesn't want to be without a man. So, she doesn't protest. I think that kind of relationship creates a lot of tension."

Such affairs cause men pain too. If their extramarital relationship is indiscreet enough to call attention to itself, they may feel the weight of censorship from their families and friends. Some have genuine remorse about the pain they've caused and about having let their affairs "get out of hand."

Most men who get involved with other women don't deliberately set out to destroy their marriages. In fact, the period after the fourth stage of backlash may represent a loss of control for men who are getting pressure from their wives and from their lovers.

Women, of course, have affairs too and many of them suffer from the same feelings of neglect and abandonment as their husbands. Others seek lovers in retaliation for their husband's dalliance. Most, however, look to extramarital affairs to provide them with a love relationship in which they don't have to be adversarial. Often, their burnout has put them in touch with their own human and sexual needs, feelings that had been supressed. When female self-esteem is low, many look to bolster their self-confidence with the attentions of another man.

Women say they have affairs with the kind of high-powered, self-assured men they wish their husbands were. Others just want to spend time with someone who will be nice to them. They want attention, excitement, and the intimacy lacking in their marriages. "When I did have an affair," said a woman from Alabama, whose salary and position far exceeded her husband's, "it was with a person whose position was more prestigious than my husband's. He was good to me. We could talk about a variety of subjects without his becoming intimidated because I knew something he didn't. It was nice to have someone on my level. And, of course, we didn't have any real problems, so the sex was great. The relationship just sort of faded. I really wasn't ready to make a strong commitment. It came down to the fact that I didn't want to leave my husband."

The double standard operates even when wives take on lovers. Women still can't come and go with the same amount of freedom as their husbands. Most husbands won't tolerate their wives coming in at three o'clock in the morning, whereas many women have been socialized to keep quiet about their husbands' late hours. Many women fear that their husbands will react violently if their wives' indiscretion is discovered. Perhaps even more deep-seated is the sense of guilt many women have regarding extramarital affairs. Finally, even part-time male lovers aren't adept at subordinating themselves to a woman's schedule and her demands. Ultimately, the same conditions that threaten her marriage tend to make a woman's affair short-lived and unsatisfactory. The complications deter many women from having affairs even though they may want a lover.

Because the cultural expectation is that women will maintain homes and preserve marriages, many feel they've personally failed when their marriages don't work. At the same time, confronting the societal stigma of being alone is a mammoth psychological struggle. At the end of the fourth stage, most are emotionally battered. According to experts, women who discover their husbands' infidelities go through the four stages of loss commonly associated with accepting the death of a loved one: denial, anger and depression, guilt, and finally acceptance. Afraid of being alone, many desperately hold on to their relationship. "I tried really hard to make things work after I discovered my husband's affair," said Carolyn, an interior designer. "I tried more than he did. All I wanted him to do was reaffirm his commitment to the marriage, but he was so confused he couldn't. I clung to him. I saw having him as affirmation that I was a good woman."

Male infidelity wounds women, damaging their self-esteem and self-confidence in much the same way men say they have been hurt by their wives' neglect. Many women are shocked when their guilty husbands refuse to grovel and beg for forgiveness, instead placing the blame on the wife's lack of attentiveness. More than the act itself, the aftermath of infidelity, so full of accusations and counteraccusations, is what essentially brings dual-career couples to the brink.

"When I found out about my husband's affair, I was crushed," said Marilyn, an accountant for a large firm in Chicago. There was a frenzied week where Marilyn screamed, cursed, stormed, and threw things. Her outrage subsided as she listened incredulously as Jeffrey explained that it was her fault he'd chosen to be with another woman, her fault because she didn't want to act like a real wife. "I guess I was kind of masochistic. I kept asking my husband, 'Why did this happen?' Well, for the several months we stayed together after I found out about his other woman, he told me every single reason why it happened. He tried to make me feel it was all my fault. He said, 'You're never home. You don't do this. You don't do that.' Everything from my not cooking to my not making love often enough. I got very angry and resentful. I didn't want him to ask me to do anything. I became very belligerent. 'You want me to get what? Get it yourself!' that was my attitude. His affair really tore our marriage apart, but more than that, it tore me apart. By the time I walked away from that relationship, I had no concept of myself as a woman. When we separated, I didn't have any confidence in myself. It took years for me to recover."

When women doubt their womanliness as men have come to doubt their manliness, two emotionally depleted people quickly reach an impasse that presents only two choices: to end the marriage or work hard to rebuild it.

PART THREE

Working On It

9

The Decision to Stay

More than any other institution, the American marriage has been most intimately affected by the changes wrought by the women's movement. Largely uninitiated in the ways of sexual equality, without substantial role models to guide them, with no societal supports in place to assist them, couples struggle, falter, and many fail. Is there any wonder that dual-career marriages become battlegrounds? If anyone could have predicted the emotional war zone that lay ahead, men and women might have been prepared to cope with it and more marriages might have been saved.

At the end of the fourth stage of backlash, there may be precious little to salvage. Marriage partners no longer trust each other and many feel more anger and pain than love.

Feeling trapped and crazy, couples may consider ending their marriages. Yet, separation is neither an easy choice nor an automatic one, as people sifting through the realities of divorce begin to realize.

In an era when two paychecks are often essential for keeping homes afloat, both men and women must consider the financial impact of splitting up. During the first quarter of 1998, women earned 76 cents for every dollar men earned.[20] The "feminization of poverty," a term coined in the seventies, underscores which sex bears the financial brunt of divorce. For many mothers the cost of childcare alone would rip through their salaries. While husband backlash assaults their psyches, corporate backlash keeps many women firmly in their places. If women haven't usurped the "last hired, first fired" domain of black workers, they have created their own category: cheapest hired, least promoted. Many women, despite the current greater opportunities across the board, feel a real lack of upward mobility within their own companies. When confronted with the financial aspects of splitting up, they ask themselves: Can I afford to do this?

Men, too, can't ignore the dollars and cents of divorce. Although women worry more about not having enough money without a partner, men also must face the realities of tightening their belts if they lose a spouse's earnings. When

---

[20] Bureau of Labor Statistics, 1998.

their wives earn just as much or more than they do, men must dramatically reduce their standard of living. If part of the problem in backlash marriages has been the wife's independent use of her own money, one of the ironies for men considering separating from these women is the negative consequences of being without that money. A few men must even consider a loss in social status if they divorce, because their wives' jobs are more prestigious than their own.

Because most husbands do outearn their wives, men, more than women, worry about what will be taken away from them in a divorce. "I had a lot of anxiety about leaving my wife," said Carl, a tax attorney. "We had acquired quite a bit together. We had a beautiful home, two cars, nice furniture. I was worried that she'd take everything. At one point, I even broke off the relationship with my lover because of the financial implications. As it turned out, my wife got quite a bit. I had to move into a much smaller home."

Many couples have gone deeply into debt during their marriages, as they've assumed a life-style that is financed by plastic. Men fear they will be saddled with the bulk of the debt. They say that the courts still favor the women in divorce cases and fear huge settlements will cost them most of their capital.

Children are a major consideration for men and women. Even in these days of no-fault divorces, many unhappy couples stay together because of their children. They pose the most serious implications for women, since mothers are so often awarded custody. They may have to radically change their lives. Some will need to consider moving to a less expensive neighborhood and enrolling their children in less than satisfactory schools. Many women who could cope with a dip in standards for themselves are reluctant to subject their children to such a change. They also doubt their ability to rear their children alone. They have read the statistics about even "good" fathers abandoning their children once couples divorce and they are frightened it will happen to them.

Men are concerned about the emotional impact of separation on their children too. "After a number of years of marriage, things were bad enough that I was ready to leave," said Jonathan, 42, a writer. "My son was a major consideration. He and I have a pretty close relationship. We still have a 'tuck in and kiss' ritual each night. I would miss that relationship. I couldn't be a weekend father. Being a single person represented freedom, but I wanted my son to grow up in an intact family. The family setting is extremely important to him. And I didn't want some other man playing dad to my son, undoing and redoing everything I've taught him." Jonathan had heard horror stories about women manipulating their ex-husbands with their children. He feared becoming a victim. And, like many women, he was worried about a drop in the standard of living of his child.

Perhaps even more traumatic than the financial implications is the emotional impact of breaking up. Without a marriage, many women feel invalidated; confronting the societal stigma of being alone is a mammoth psychological struggle.

Particularly for those who went from their parents' home to marriage, the thought of dating is frightening. They're afraid of being lonely or sexually exploited. And they fear being infected with a sexually transmitted disease.

Men have many of the same concerns. While society doesn't dub men failures if their marriages don't work, some men may feel an overwhelming sense of loss, particularly if they were reared with conservative values. If the men have an extramarital relationship, they may not feel secure enough about the other woman to risk leaving their wives. Even though they are dissatisfied, marriage gives many men a sense of order they fear losing. No matter what the other woman has promised, she is the unknown. And while those relationships have meant sexual gratification and ego satisfaction, for many men the thought of their wives finding similar satisfaction with other men is devastating.

Some men who consider separation face another set of problems. Like women, they wonder and worry about their ability to attract members of the opposite sex. If they are shy or married very young, they may suffer anxiety in social situations. Some may feel they are incapable of maintaining a monogamous relationship, if they perceive themselves failures in their marriages. They also fear the sexually transmitted diseases that are prevalent today. Others simply feel uncomfortable about becoming a bachelor again. They don't have the skills to create a home and they worry about the mechanics of taking care of themselves. In fact, so preferred is the married state for men that the great majority of divorced men soon remarry.

Married men appear more stable to many corporations. "I was really anxious when I went in to tell my boss that my wife and I were separating," said John, the energy manager. "The company is very conservative and most of the managers are married. I was due for a promotion and I was a little scared that my personal problems would have an adverse effect on my changes for advancement."

With all the deterrents, it's a wonder so many couples do separate. Yet, there are times when there is no chance of saving a backlash marriage. "After I discovered his affairs and he became physically abusive, I realized the marriage was over. I just wanted to end it," said Sylvia, the television producer.

Leaving a backlash marriage, however, is no cure for the underlying problem. Walking out, without dealing with the issues, almost guarantees that backlash will follow you. When men leave their professional wives, even for women who appear to be willingly subordinate to them, it doesn't make the issue of backlash disappear. There is no guarantee that the passive "other woman" will remain so. The man who feels he can escape a changing society is stunned when his new woman turns out to be less traditional than she seemed. Within two years after Aurelia's ex-husband remarried a woman he thought was an earthy, mothering person, she announced she was enrolling in law school. Nick, the manager for an automobile leasing agency, and his new wife struggled over her working until two pregnancies in rapid succession forced her to stay at home. Women who run away from their marriages in search of a more liberated prince charming are chastened to find their dates just as marked by their early socialization process as their husbands.

Working things out isn't easy. If backlash couples are going to stay together happily, they must begin the process of confronting the problematic issues and coping with the anger that has splintered their marriages. To turn a backlash marriage around means admitting guilt, hammering out terms, attempting to change. In short, it requires commitment.

Couples who opt to stay and repair their marriages seem to have a better chance if the people genuinely like each other, regardless of what has happened. Before the necessary compromises can be made, though, husbands and wives must begin to communicate with each other. It seems so obvious to repeat that old phrase but, in fact, where these problems have been worked out, communication seems to have been the key.

It is very clear to anyone around them when a couple communicates successfully: they have visibly achieved intimacy, closeness, and a deeper sharing, caring, and understanding of one another. Couples like this aren't always happy with one another, but usually each partner is aware of how the other is feeling. They don't try to hide what is painful or frightening behind a wall of silence or indifference. Communication fosters growth in the relationship as well as personal growth of two individuals. For marriages where communication is good, two people are each other's sounding boards; they enlarge each other's worlds.

Though it's easy to recognize good communicators, how they got that way is harder to pinpoint. Most people bring to their marriages a family history. If their mother and father were emotionally expressive, truthful people, most likely they are also. But one or both partners may have grown up in emotionally repressive environments. Current thinking is that males have the tendency to avoid verbalizing their feelings and often are frightened of doing so. Women, on the other hand, are thought to be overly emotional. In her book, *Intimate Strangers, Men and Women Together*, author Lillian B. Rubin aptly refers to that common perception as "the rational-man-hysterical-woman script." It's not always accurate.

"My husband and I don't talk," said a Washington federal executive. "If something is bothering him, he'll clam up. If I don't raise it, he won't. And most of the time, I won't raise an issue," she said.

Some of the women I spoke with had very intricate ways of avoiding intimacy with the men in their lives. These devices were often found in the maze of seemingly ordinary behavior. Upon closer examination, it's clear they chose to work long hours as a convenient way to avoid being close to their spouses The superwoman syndrome, painful as it is, offers an escape hatch for wives who are uncomfortable with emotional attachments.

It is apparent by their behavior that neither husbands nor wives in backlash marriages are talking to each other about the guilt, anger, and confusion they feel. Many simply don't know how. Unsure of how to reveal their true feelings and too frightened to try, they assume their partner can read their minds. Or at least they hope they can. Most couples prone to backlash have difficulty expressing verbally their emotions and needs. Sooner or later their backed-up emotions explode. Ironically, rage is the only method they have for letting off steam. For too many backlash couples, fighting is the only communication that is comfortable.

Fortunately, husbands and wives who are committed to salvaging their marriages can begin to change negative patterns. Not all successful communicators were born that way; many have learned as adults. While the dual-career marriage presents complex problems, learning to communicate effectively can be the first step in healing a relationship torn apart by backlash.

Couples in the final stages of backlash need to detach from their anger in order to create a space in which dialogue is possible. For most busy professional couples, simply finding an unscheduled moment, time when they can talk in a relaxed manner with their spouse, is a challenge, as is creating an environment that is conducive to sharing innermost thoughts. Learning the techniques of what to say and how to say it will be helpful, but the important task is just to begin the process of getting closer through words.

Beyond talking with each other, couples must focus on other forms of communications, including the sexual. And both men and women who are interested in achieving genuine intimacy must learn to listen. Opening up to another human being can be a fearsome prospect, but for those committed to ending the state of siege in their homes, it is the only recourse. Some couples may need the help of a trained therapist. Others can begin the process themselves. But only after they hoist a white flag.

People scream and yell when they're fighting; they accuse and blame. They don't communicate. Effective communication can't take place in an atmosphere of hostility and anger. Old patterns must be changed. Husbands and wives who are embroiled in the last stages of backlash must call a truce. They must *specifically* agree to an official time out. This requires stepping away from the emotional investment they have in marital conflict and deciding how much of their relationship can be salvaged and how best to rebuild the marriages. The husband and wife may not be able to coordinate motivation; one may be more anxious than the other. Still, the refusal of one partner to engage in hostilities usually moves both toward creating an environment in which talk can begin.

Sometimes, however, truces aren't dependent on either spouse; they are shaped by events. "My marriage got really bad in 1981, to the point where I was ready to leave. Then our child died in a car accident. Everything stood still for both of us. We were completely numb. We couldn't feel anger toward each other anymore. Our daughter's death forced us to stop being each other's enemy," said Harold, a musician.

Fortunately, most couples don't have to experience the

death of a beloved child to compel them to end the state of siege in their homes. They may, however, have to separate temporarily in order to find relief from the tensions that are plaguing their relationship.

"My husband told me in November that he was having an affair and I left in December. I needed to put some space between us," said Grace, the department store executive. "I got a promotion and I moved outside of the city. Where I lived was very isolated, because no one I knew was anywhere near me. I needed time alone to begin realizing who I was and what I wanted. After almost a year, my husband told me that he'd ended his affair. We began dating and ultimately we got back together."

Other couples report having managed to "disengage" while still living together. Husbands and wives can plan separate vacations, evenings away from each other, and make efforts to limit contact with their partner. Then, once the environment is less charged emotionally, they can attempt to learn the process of expressing their feelings to each other.

"For husbands and wives attempting to improve communication, the goal is to know, understand, respond to and share with a partner," said Maryann Poster, a psychologist and family therapist who at the time practiced in Los Angeles. Poster suggests that "knowing yourself is important, because the more you know about yourself, the easier it is to make requests or respond to another person. People need to be very clear and specific when they talk with each other. . . . Otherwise, they respond to what they're projecting.

Finally, spouses have to be willing to learn what their partner wants. They have to be willing to take risks and do something different."

"Couples say they want to talk, but what they tend to do is avoid contact," said Nancy Steiny, a family therapist practicing at the Southern California Counseling Center in Los Angeles. "Couples need to set aside a specific time to talk that's a routine, that they do on a daily basis. When husbands and wives are both working and they have children, they can think of three thousand reasons never to have time to discuss things. Talking together has to be a habit. If you wait to save whatever it is you want to talk about for signals that the other person is ready to talk, well, obviously you may be beyond it." Beginning conversations may border on the mundane, but discussions on current events may eventually lead to discourse about feelings.

Effective communication brings couples closer; the wrong words can alienate. There is a right and wrong way to call attention to dissatisfactions. Many experts advise couples to tell their partners how they feel about problems by using the pronoun "I," as opposed to "you." The difference is clear: "You never help me with the housework," is antagonistic, pointing the finger of blame at the other partner. "I feel that I need more help with the housework," is less likely to anger the listener. Using "I" says the speaker is taking responsibility for his or her own behavior and encourages the listener to do the same.

One of the most important steps toward intimacy is to

deal with problems as they occur. Stored anger and hurt feelings tend to become exaggerated over time. Avoiding the trap of trying to solve all problems at once, limiting the discussion to one or two current issues, and sticking to concrete facts and feelings are all important if behavior is going to change.

In the beginning, verbal communication may be difficult, particularly if couples have avoided talking for a long time. Getting in touch with nonverbal cues may help ease the tension. Body language and sexual expression communicate what many couples can't say in words. A smile, gesture or touch, a particular tone of voice can often convey what people feel uncomfortable saying. Sexual expression can also give clear messages about what a person is feeling. Sex is the only emotional outlet many men allow themselves. Women should be aware that their husbands' need for sex is also his desire to feel connected and loved.

Couples who want to share intimacy have learned that patience is required. "I can't explain how my wife and I mended our marriage," said Steve, 37, a salesman. "We both really wanted things to work out, but we didn't figure it would take us as long as it did for us to start caring about each other again.

"We used to have to create an artificial environment to talk when we first began our attempt to patch things up. If we were at home, the kids had to be in bed, the television off, the lights just so. Or else, we'd have to go out to some upscale restaurant where the ambiance was perfect for conversation. It wasn't natural. My wife and I seemed incapable of just casually falling into a discussion about anything meaningful. Our conversations were rather stilted at first, because they were so orchestrated. We'd both get frustrated, but we kept right on stumbling along.

"It was depressing at times and I guess since we were both going through it we began to reach out to each other. We couldn't synchronize our low periods. When I was up, she was down. I learned to look at her and tell how she was feeling. I started giving her little hugs when I knew she was depressed. I guess I'm more into nonverbal communication. Then she began telling me when she wasn't feeling okay.

"Within the last couple of years, we've really begun to break through all the formality that was restricting us at first. Now we have meaningful conversations in bed, in the car, right in front of our child. I really value that because now we talk about the stuff that used to get shoved aside. It's not a case of me against her, like it used to be. I feel the need to be less defensive. We're closer."

When couples talk at regularly scheduled intervals and as trust grows, they are able to disclose the emotions that are at the root of backlash.

"It took my husband several years to feel comfortable enough with me and with our relationship to open up and admit to me that he was afraid of my career success," said Grace. "Very slowly, it began to come out how he felt about my job. He told me he felt he was competing with me and losing. He felt he wasn't keeping up with me and he hated that feeling. It made him feel unmanly."

According to Audrey Chapman, a family therapist who specializes in female stress, "Women have to begin telling men some of the downs of the professional world. They have to start sharing the sexism, the missed promotions, the tension they feel when they have to choose between work and family. They have to describe for their husbands the pain of trying to be superwomen."

Perhaps the most important part of any communication is listening—giving silent, undivided attention to the person who is speaking. That may be the most difficult part of a reconciliation. "I had to force myself to learn to really listen to my wife," admitted Harold. "And she seemed able to listen to everyone else but me. After my daughter died I really had difficulty coping with the grief. I was unable to talk about it or cry. I guess I thought that would be unmasculine. I walked around feeling incredibly angry and I guess everyone could tell that I was having a difficult time. I took a friend's suggestion and went to an Elisabeth Kübler-Ross seminar that lasted a week. People were split up into groups and I learned that I was able to talk in the group. I was also forced to listen to other people talking about their grief. In that week, I began learning to be an effective listener and when I left the seminar that skill carried over into my marriage."

Listening is difficult because the listener eventually has to give some feedback and risk a response that may resume old tensions. Many experts recommend that people simply paraphrase the statements of the person who is speaking. To the husband who is describing an unfair boss, a wife can say, "I hear you saying that your boss has mistreated you." The "I hear you" phrase acknowledges what's been said and at the same time avoids antagonizing with criticism.

Men and women come together because of mutual needs. Backlash, burnout, and hostility result when partners perceive they are being denied, even though in many cases those needs were never clearly stated. As communication improves, husbands and wives are able to tell each other what is essential for their happiness.

"Darryl, my husband, revealed a lot to me when we finally started opening up to one another," said Roxanne, the mother of two young children. She had recently started a new position in city administration in a large southern city. "He felt like he was competing with me for my time, since I put in long hours and then I had so many meetings at night. It was difficult for me to compromise. I love the job; it's like being on stage. I love having power and getting accolades. I have to admit that my ego was the biggest stress in terms of juggling two careers. I liked to be out. But I have compromised. I'm much more willing to say that I don't want to go back and put in such long hours. At my current job, I feel as though I'm on part time and that's okay. This year I've said to my community organizations that I can meet during the morning, and at noon, but not at night, because I have a previous engagement. There are things that I'd like to attend that are held between five and seven in the evening, but for this point in my life I choose to spend that time with my husband and children. And in return, I'm getting a husband who spends more time with our children."

To resolve the backlash problem, couples must hammer out compromises that satisfy male demands for a more traditional woman and female demands for a more egalitarian man. The issues of backlash have to be brought out of the closet before solutions can be reached. Husbands and wives can begin to cope fairly with chores by: 1. getting household help if they can afford it; 2. involving older children in housework; 3. making contracts and verbal agreements for chore assignments; 4. lowering their own expectations of how clean and orderly their homes must be. Men can be taught what equal parenting is all about and women can relinquish clinging dependency, but only if these issues are discussed.

Once people talk, they can be amazingly creative and resourceful. A recent *Los Angeles Times* article described a young couple who share the job of high-school teacher. Since 1981, they have each alternated teaching one year and staying at home with their young children the next year. When one parent works, the other takes care of their children. They plan to continue the arrangement for several more years, until their youngest child is school age.

While job sharing isn't new, what is interesting is the way one couple was able to forge a compromise. According to the article, when the two teachers married the wife requested that they both use both their last names. The husband was so upset at what his father might say, he couldn't speak for an hour. And yet, three years later, he was able to agree to an arrangement that would threaten the masculinity of many men.

It is clear that along with the ability to communicate, these people were able to think of manhood and womanhood in new terms. The success of their compromises rests on their clear understanding that there are male and female traits that must be expressed. Expansive definitions of masculinity and femininity are needed, not just for the sake of marriage, but for individual growth.

10

Blending Femininity and Feminism

Not long after my divorce, Walter, one of my favorite male friends, paid me a visit. His marriage of six years was rocky and he laid the blame on his wife's lack of instinctual domesticity. "What's wrong with a woman wanting to stay at home and take care of her children? Whatever happened to that kind of woman?" he asked, his voice almost plaintive with sincerity. It sounded like whining to me. I was getting him a can of beer and I banged it down hard on the kitchen counter. Walter's head jolted upright. In the old days I'd been his ally and confidante; he hadn't expected me ever to turn on him.

"She woke up," I said tersely. "She found out she gets more respect when she makes some money. Her own money." My memory isn't clear, but it wouldn't surprise me if at that point I launched into a diatribe about the wages of housewifery being poverty in a woman's old age when the guy deserts her to take up with some bimbo.

When my friend left my house he had a dazed, shell-shocked look. Walter had, unfortunately, stumbled into one of my explosively bitter moods. During the months following my divorce anything that smacked of female dependency or need for a man met with my sharp veto. I wanted to be able to do completely without men, be totally independent. Why should any man expect a woman to sit home and take care of him and some kids when she could go out and set the world on fire with her own achievements? I wasn't ever going to be trapped by domesticity again.

Two weeks after my conversation with Walter, I had a huge party, a gathering of the most eclectic group of artists, writers, and philosophers I could find. I invited friends, friends of friends, people I admired from afar, announcing to everyone that I wanted to start a network, an organization of like-minded noncorporate types who would nurture and sustain each other as we pursued our goals. My guests, all single men and women, sat around my small living room and exchanged stories of artistic struggles. I basked in an intellectual glow. Achievement, I thought to myself, that's what makes life worthwhile.

The group never met again, although I sincerely thought we would, but that party marked my debut as a single woman with intense aspirations. Now that I was divorced I could write until the wee, wee hours and no one would tell me to come to bed. I would enrich myself with lectures, plays, and books and learn as much as I pleased. Above all, I would not allow myself to be defined or limited by any man. It was symbolic that I didn't cook at my first party as I had done when I entertained as a wife. I served pretzels and potato chips and other store-bought goodies. I was breaking away from the stove. Fast food, that was my speed.

If in the heat of my antimale passion someone could have shown me a picture of my life not long after, if I could have seen myself clamoring for dates, slipping back into dependence and even subservience, I would have been appalled. The full circle I was to travel was even more astonishing. Three years later, Ms. Fast Foods stood in front of a stove, stirring at least four different pots, while the man in my life, my future husband, reclined on his sofa. What was amazing wasn't that I was cooking for a man again, but that I no longer resisted the act as a betrayal of feminist principles.

It felt natural cooking for a man. Stevie Wonder was playing in the background. My daughter was laughing over some silliness with my fiancé. The scene was blissfully domestic and I was happier than I'd been in a long, long time. Trying to please the man I cared for was satisfying. Maybe part of my pleasure was knowing that this particular man would set the table, clear it, and wash the dishes. Maybe not. More than his doing his share, what was personally fulfilling to me was the relish with which he ate the meal I'd prepared. To be honest, I enjoyed being the cause of his satisfaction every bit as much as I liked researching magazine articles and seeing my name in print. That admission, as unremarkable as it seems today, coming after several years of denial and suppression, made me feel as though I'd rediscovered some missing part of myself.

In a past issue of *Savvy*, there is an intriguing photograph: two women stare hostilely at each other at the entrance of a revolving door, one coming out, the other going in. The one who is leaving is the total embodiment of the working woman, from her pin-striped suit to her precise, upswept hairdo, little tie, and briefcase. Her corporate armor says she is sophisticated, intelligent, and decisive, an important woman who makes the world take notice. Clad in jeans and a sweater, her hair windblown, struggling with a toddler, the other one is definitely a homemaker, a woman perceived by many as being traditional, maternal, a woman whose station in life is determined not by her achievements, but by those of her husband.

The title of the article, "Women at Odds," describes the growing animosity between homemakers and working women. It is often a large-scale and public battle between the politics of the antifeminist new right and such women's groups as the National Organization for Women. Much less publicized is the battle of those two forces as it is waged inside the psyches of today's working women.

I lived through such a war. Deep within me, two very different and equally powerful components of my own being were fighting for supremacy in my life. Despite my sassy declaration to my friend Walter and to other men, inside my head, the homemaker in me wouldn't disappear. That woman was rooted there, whether I wanted her or not. Although I professed to be totally independent, my assertive, achieving self was constantly duking it out with the nurturing, more dependent, "feminine" woman within me. And I was feeling the blows. It took me three years to realize I needed *all* the components of my womanhood to be whole.

For years women have been trapped by history's truncated image that limited them to homemaking. Only recently were women able to shed that definition, but in retrospect, they exchanged one bind for another. The women's movement, reacting to history, imposed an image of the woman who could do whatever men did, if she were given an equal opportunity. Neither picture was complete, but women were forced to choose between them to define their identity. No matter which role model they picked, they were penalized. Working women feel guilty both for not spending enough time with their children and for not working as hard at their jobs as their male counterparts. Homemakers feel devalued because they don't earn money in a society that measures personal success by income and also because they fear their mothering abilities aren't good enough. Both homemakers and working women experience the stress that stems from denying and suppressing an important part of themselves.

Everyone seems to be demanding that women choose: either, or. Work *or* stay home. Be nurturing *or* be a career woman. Men are apparently threatened by the idea that anybody can do it all, no less women. Women are *afraid* to let both sides of themselves flower for fear that the two can't coexist—that if they cook dinner it will undermine their ability to pick stocks.

Yet, the dilemma of backlash cries out for women who value the combination of femininity and independence, who can be soft and strong, achieving and supportive. "The healthy relationship permits change," says Laurie Klein Evans. "In that kind of marriage, the very strong career woman is allowed to come home and say, 'I want to be babied.' Unfortunately, most couples don't have the fluidity to move from one fit to another." If working women want to resurrect their marriages and minimize backlash, they are going to have to rediscover the parts of themselves they've been suppressing and take their whole selves into all areas of their lives. They are going to have to both manage their careers and their personal lives. To do so, they must begin to address the issues making it difficult for them to integrate their femininity and feminism.

Up until the landmark Civil Rights Act of 1964, professions where females predominated—teaching, nursing, and social work—capitalized on women's capacity to nurture. Indeed, women were deemed to be more suited to those kinds of work because of their femininity. But now in America's corporations, female expression has been outlawed. Women have learned that their admittance to corporate America wasn't an invitation to bring their sexual/cultural selves to the workplace; it carried a slippery imperative to conform to male corporate culture.

What has happened in the more than twenty years since the Civil Rights Act is that in order to succeed, many women, already convinced they must deliberately masculinize their dress, speech, method of working, and how they express leadership and emotions, have also adopted the male value system that consciously and unconsciously denigrates female cultural expression in the workplace. While a few women attempt to play the new game the old way—trading on their sexuality or acting the little girl as a means of succeeding in their companies—most don't. Research reveals that the young women who are ascending in fields that were traditionally male exhibit more of the characteristics associated with male leadership than do men. A "macho female" has emerged, a suited and tied individual who succeeds in her job by making her male co-workers and superiors feel culturally comfortable with her, even though she may feel very uncomfortable herself. "Many men have told me I think like a man and respond like a man," said Rita, the owner of a successful janitorial service in Philadelphia. "At my business, I'm a no-nonsense person. I have to be."

"I felt I had to outperform everybody," confessed one female corporate executive. "I was an eighty-hour-a-week worker."

The irony is that research is beginning to show a greater need for undiluted female-style management, and in particular that national leadership needs to reflect a greater balance of feminine and masculine style. The major difference between the masculine, or "alpha style," and the feminine, or "beta style," is that alpha is more direct and seeks a clear win-or-lose outcome for a given problem. Beta is more concerned with the quality of life and not necessarily a clear win. While both styles are present in both sexes, sex role expectations have made males adopt more alpha attitudes and females more beta. Male-run corporations have, up to now, used alpha management styles, but heads of major companies are now investing money in developing beta-style thinking in their executives. Findings indicate that this female style is needed to deal with problems that require a broader perspective. Accepting a style of work that isn't comfortable makes success elusive. Many women don't cut the corporate mustard, not because they can't master their jobs—studies have shown that women are more methodical, conscientious workers than their male counterparts—but because they can't switch to "male think." There is a need for a certain amount of conformity in big business; a multiplicity of business styles and techniques might prove confusing and counterproductive. But corporate America might profit from a management style that gives voice to a greater range of emotional expression and women's more developed ability to be empathetic with people. Making use of a female-centered style would benefit men as well as women in business.

In addition to the *value* to business of the feminine mode, women can no longer afford work identities that impair their marriages and reinforce the message that their own sexual orientation and value system aren't valid. Choosing to be a macho female takes a terrible toll on women's lives. Although males still have higher mortality rates from most major diseases and women still outlive men by more than ten years, since the 1970s women have been "catching up." Since 1968, deaths from heart disease have decreased faster for men than for women. Currently, one in ten American women 45 to 64 years of age has some form of heart disease, and this increases to one in four women over 65.[21] Between the years 1965–1978, 30 percent of all women smoked. Almost 23 percent of all American adult women (22.6 million) are now smokers. While fewer women than men smoke in general, it is estimated that in the year 2000, women are smoking at the same rate as men. Women who quit smoking relapse for different reasons than men. Stress, weight control, and negative emotions lead to relapse among women.[22] Federal health officials estimate that one out of every three Americans with a drinking problem is a woman. These statistics are a reflection of the ever-increasing pressure women are feeling as they move into what used to be "a man's world." They are also a result of women struggling to maintain the delicate balance of being homemakers and workers.

Some women are acknowledging to themselves, their hus-

---

[21] From National Heart, Lung and Blood Institute, National Institute of Health Publication (originally printed 1995, reprinted in 1998).

[22] From American Lung Association, Fact Sheet on Women and Smoking.

bands, and their bosses that they need time to care for their families. Rather than struggling to be superwomen, a few working wives are beginning to consider cutting back on workloads that spell overload. "When I interviewed for my current job, the president told me, 'Well, I'm very impressed with you. Now, tell me about your downside.' And I said, 'I leave every day at five o'clock, no matter what. I have a marriage and a family and I'm not willing to see either go down the tubes.' And I've stuck to that decision," said Dena, an architect.

Fathers are also attempting to balance the demands of careers and children.

"Jean already had a child from another marriage," said Bob, a New York city planner. "I wanted a baby more than she did and part of our deal was that I'd take a big share of the responsibilities. The sitter couldn't come in one day last week and the baby had a sore throat, so I called in to say I wouldn't be able to get in to the office." The question remains whether businesses will recognize the importance of stable family lives for employees.

In a sense the ability of women to blend femininity with their assertive selves hinges on minimizing the paranoia of big business and that of their own husbands. Women say they fear the repercussions to their careers if they express their femininity at work. They must convince the companies they work for that the bottom line won't be adversely affected if the workplace is somewhat feminized. At the same time, if they are to diminish the backlash coming from their spouses, they must convince their men they have nothing to fear from a professionally powerful wife. Women can win in both arenas if they believe they have a right to a career *and* family success. There is really no contradiction in being both a successful professional and a loving mate. It's what women have been trying to get from men for a long time. Now, *both* sexes need to concentrate on *both* factors.

Rena, a journalist, has given herself permission to be fulfilled as a wife and writer. She recognizes that the marriage she describes as "strong" enables her to succeed in her profession. "My tensions aren't in the marriage; that's where my support comes from. The nearly two years I've been married have been the most productive of my life. I've written more, gotten more accomplished professionally, and made more connections.

"I always knew I'd work and have a family. As a child I had this fantasy. I'd have a house with a white picket fence and I would be a lawyer. My office would be right next to the baby's room. I would hear the baby cry and excuse myself from clients to go change her. My picture of a husband was Walter Pidgeon. He and Greer Garson had done a movie about Marie Curie. In it, he gave up his career to help her find radium. He was on his way to buy his wife some amethyst earrings for her birthday and got run over by a horse and carriage. I cried for three days. That was my image of a marriage."

Rena's fantasy has matured over the years, but her early conditioning led her to choose a man who was genuinely interested in her development and did not need her to mother him. Her own husband isn't quite as self-sacrificing as Mr. Curie, but he is understanding about deadlines, doesn't complain when she gives her full attention to writing, and isn't insecure because she outearns him.

Although both Rena and her husband enjoy their careers, their priority is the marriage. "We make time for each other," said Rena succinctly.

The best strategy women can use to minimize backlash is to convey to their husbands how much they love and need them in language men understand.

Sometimes backlash can be avoided by trying to anticipate and defuse the situations that cause it. For example, a husband who does not feel comfortable with his wife's career may see it this way: his wife wakes up in the morning, gets all dressed up, and rushes to an office he's never seen, where she does work he knows little about, and where she gets a lot of attention from other men. No wonder he feels threatened.

Demystifying her job may forestall a lot of problems in this woman's home. She can tell her husband in advance when she and her co-workers—some of them male—are going to be working late together or traveling. Introducing her husband to the men with whom she works at office parties or other less formal occasions can also be a help. Some women told me their husbands didn't like them to talk about their jobs at home, to "bring their office home with them"; others report that it was very helpful to make it clear that the wife's career is at least as problematic as the husband's.

In those dual-career marriages that are happiest, couples seem to view female as well as male success as the family's success. Women in these marriages make obvious the gains the family reaps from their earning power by sharing their wealth equitably with their husbands. They don't expect to be excused from financial responsibility or dirty work because they are women.

The other striking characteristic of women who seem to retain their femininity and blend it with assertiveness, is that they don't allow their jobs or even anger at their husbands to come into their beds and ruin their sex lives. Men, of course, share culpability when marital sexuality sags; professional counseling may be needed to uncover the emotional and psychological reasons for a couple's lack of libido. Both husbands and wives need to address the issues that seem to be common in two-career families. Sex doesn't take care of itself. In marriages that seem to be doing well, couples have made sex a priority. Busy but happy dual-career couples seem to know how to set aside times for intimacy and to keep those times clear by using any resources available: babysitters, fast foods, weekends away. In particular, many professional women need to take the time to tune into their own sexuality. It also seems to be important to create a transition period between the tension of work and shifting gears to the personal. Without that time, sex can be a tense, unpleasant experience for men and women. Both husbands and wives cheat themselves when they make professional achievements an excuse for neglecting their sexual lives. There would be fewer unhappy marriages if people realized they don't have to choose between personal and professional success. The two go hand in hand.

Women can say they'll refuse to be superwomen, but in order for that frenzied martyr to disappear, men must believe and communicate that she is just as much a liability for them as for women.

In other cases women may have to help men discover the kind of relationships they really want. The majority of men I spoke to seem to have less of a problem with sexual equality than with their inability to feel masculine without wives who provide the supports and services they've been reared to believe "real men" deserve. In other words, most men don't have a problem with their wives working late; but it is hard for them to feel manly when they come into an empty house. Their fathers came home to a smiling, encouraging wife who had dinner ready—and that is part of what defined them as "Daddy." In other words, if women listen closely, they will hear what men are not saying. Their husbands may seem to be asking them to cook and clean, but they are really asking for help in finding a new way to feel masculine. They are seeking the same kind of wholeness that women are after.

Female liberation can't be accomplished while the male psyche is in chains. Women who can encourage men to take another look at being liberated may achieve changes in their relationship that they would not achieve with the political tactics of the early sixties and seventies. It isn't likely that female anger and male guilt will be the catalyst for a permanent change in society. Women need to encourage men toward the direction of their own liberation, to resurrect in some instance and conceive in others, their own movement.

11

The Free Men of the Eighties

The odor of savory spices greeted me inside Kevin and Maria's renovated co-op in a working-class section of New York. Everything about Kevin and Maria seemed well blended, from the way they could talk about work problems while parenting their ten-year-old son, Juan, to their neatly combined home and small television production studio. They seemed to effortlessly split the chores—Maria cooking and Kevin setting the table. The couple's almost blissful equality belies the fact that they began their relationship burdened with the weight of the sexist acculturation of their childhoods. They both wrestled with the limitations of gender. Maria's middle-class Colombian upbringing had prepared her for a life where men were in charge and women submitted to them, but she got a lot of help from the women's movement and was supported by individual women who were also struggling toward change. It was Kevin, a third-generation, working-class Irish-American, who had the far lonelier and more difficult struggle. Virtually unaided, he opted to overcome the role modeling of male dominance he'd witnessed in his childhood and to distance himself from many of the values he'd been exposed to as a young boy, not the least of which was the sexism he saw in his parents' marriage.

"My childhood was horrible," Kevin said flatly, the rhythms of his native New York punctuating each word. An artist and independent television producer, he has the look and sound of blue-collar America, a younger, more florid version of Archie Bunker, complete with a Brooklyn bellow. His appearance notwithstanding, Kevin's sensibilities and résumé more closely resemble the yuppie experience, although he doesn't have a college degree. "My father treated my mother like shit and he was constantly abusive to her. She was a traditional wife, always complaining that my father didn't make enough money, and he ordered my mother around like a slave. He was always on her to do this, do that. I hated the way they related."

Kevin's childhood memories are the flip side of *Leave It to Beaver*, and underscore the kind of sexual polarization and hostility that often take place in traditional marriages. Even as a youngster Kevin rejected the imprinting of his upbringing. "I always thought it was unfair that women got treated the way they did." He claims he didn't see his father as the winner or leader in his marriage, or view the role of domineering male as an enviable one. Kevin didn't want to grow up and be the kind of man his father was; he thought of him as an oppressor. Yet, although Kevin believed he had detached from his upbringing early in his life, in his first marriage he was stunned when he saw patterns of female subservience and male dominance emerge.

"Kevin's first wife decided that she was going to dedicate herself to him," Maria told me, her soft, South American cadence making her words flow almost musically. "She just laid around," Kevin said quietly, disgust very evident in his tone and abbreviated gestures. "She didn't do anything at all and I just couldn't abide that kind of dependency." He also didn't like what his first marriage brought out in him. He discovered that the macho tendencies he thought he'd never identified with were, in reality, just dormant. "Out of the first relationship, I was forced to look at myself," he admitted. "I projected and said things that made me uncomfortable. I came out of that relationship in a state of hysteria."

If his first marriage underscored his abhorrence of the macho-man/dependent-woman syndrome, he was even further convinced after two years in Mexico. "The United States is one case of chauvinism, Mexico is an extraordinary case. There I began to understand machismo. Women in Mexico are treated so badly by their husbands. I remember a male doctor who threw his cigarettes on the floor in his home; his wife had to clean it up. After two years in Mexico, I didn't need a women's movement to convince me of anything.

When I met Maria I told her that any relationship that had a dependency on either side wasn't going to work. I told her if she didn't keep working and maintain her separate identity, including her own name, our relationship wasn't going to work."

Ironically, in choosing an egalitarian course for himself, he encouraged his wife to become more independent. He helped her get started in her chosen career of broadcast journalism in a more committed way than her background had prepared her to do. "When we got together, Maria had no concept of work. She wrote, but she couldn't support herself with her writing; she wasn't very productive. I picked up the technical end so she could concentrate on writing. I set up the studio in our home to make it easier for her. I've seen a change. She's much more dynamic and exciting now." Both he and Maria agree that by encouraging each other's growth, their marriage wins, as does their son, who has equal access to both his parents. Gender doesn't matter to Juan. "Kevin and I are interchangeable," said Maria.

Although Kevin recognized the paralyzing effect of female subservience and viewed women as far more victimized than men, unlike many of his peers, he didn't see men as the victor in the arrangement. "When I was a child I realized that both of my parents were irrational," he said. When he decided that he wanted more out of his life than to dominate his wife, he did so for selfish reasons. Kevin didn't choose to be egalitarian in response to the demands of a woman, but because he believed that less macho behavior offered him the most potential for his own personal growth and development.

Men like Kevin, who groped toward a new masculine value system, have had to overcome the sexism that was inculcated in them as children and break free of emotional boundaries that are part and parcel of male culture. The masculine imperative is rooted in fear. "There is homophobia around the rearing of young boys," said Dr. Alvin Poussaint, associate professor of psychiatry at the Harvard Medical School. "Parents worry if they see what they consider feminine gestures in their sons. Being a tomboy is kind of a cute phase in a female. Being a sissy is met with paranoia."

"For the most part, men are reared away from homosexuality as much as toward a positive image," said Michael Hughes, the family therapist in Los Angeles, but he believes there is another factor that limits male emotional expression. "I think the biggest problem for men overall is that most don't know how to be men. I don't get the sense that men have always been as constrained as over the last century. The industrial revolution drastically changed the relationship between father and son. In an agrarian society men and boys worked together. The industrial revolution engendered a situation where sons didn't see what their fathers did. I tend to believe this change was crucial for men."

Acting out the masculine imperative is a slow dance with death. The competitive, power-hungry, oppressive, angry, nonexpressive, nonnurturing, stoic, controlling mask that men must don leads to an emotional shutdown and hastens their physical demise. "Male patterning is a kind of oppression," suggested Dr. Poussaint, "that restricts, constrains, and limits psychological development. Males are much more narrow. They restrict themselves from participating fully in the human experience. People need to express themselves and show emotions, otherwise they're going to suffer other kinds of problems."

In almost every category of major diseases men died at a higher rate than women, according to a 1983 National Center for Health Statistics report. Now the life expectancy gap between men and women narrows significantly. Among the total population, the average American could expect to live to 76.1 years as of 1996—up from 75.8 as of 1995. Among whites, life expectancy for American men is now 73.8 years and 79.6 years for women. Black men live an average of 66.1 years, and black women live 74.2 years.[23] Some physicians attribute women's superior longevity to the greater levels of the hormone estrogen found in their bodies. Estrogen does appear to give women increased protection against some of the diseases that result more frequently in male mortality. But other experts assert that male rigidity and repression of emotional expression are major factors that increase their chances for stress-related ailments as well as alcoholism.

---

[23] From U.S. Center for Disease Control, originally from "U.S. Life Expectancy Hits New High," Sheryl Gay Stolberg, New York Times, September 12, 1997.

"I see patients with weight problems, high blood pressure, sleep disorders, and certain substance abuse problems," said Hughes. "Men are prone to beer addiction. Drinking, beer in particular, is bound culturally to images of masculinity we all grew up absorbing. Drinking has always been a part of letting off steam for men. One of the major cultural attractions of alcohol for men is that it comes with expanded boundaries. The rules of conduct and masculine behavior are altered to allow for more emotional expression than is the norm."

Men themselves concoct acceptable ways to break out of their cultural mores. Hughes believes part of males' affinity for sports—aside from athletics being a genuine source of pleasure—is generated because it allows men to be demonstrative and affectionate, something male culture forbids under ordinary circumstances. It is no coincidence that sports and alcohol are historically related. "I've observed men in groups at the ball park, drinking six beers apiece in the course of a game. Sports and alcohol facilitate camaraderie. Men have to have an excuse, a context to justify being together. The need to be together is an emotional need," said Hughes.

Individual women who demand male liberation will not accomplish that goal. And the masses of men lack the emotional fervor or political impetus to break free. But enlightened men, committed to enhancing their lives, are moving away from their self-inflicted oppression. As more men begin the painful introspection necessary to change their condition, many will realize they must break away from women who impede their progress. What cannot be ignored is the negative role some women play in sabotaging male attempts to seek a freer definition of masculinity. Unfortunately, many women are just as afraid of true male liberation as men are of female independence.

"I found out early on that a lot of the rules and regs that society lays on you will kill you if you follow them," said Edgar, 31, a banking executive. There was an air of fraternal camaraderie about this tall, thin man when we met for drinks at a quiet bar not too far from his bank in Chicago. Edgar seemed to want to talk. His words raced out as if the feelings behind them had been pent up for a long time. "The ideal of being the kind of man who conquers doesn't fit for me. I'm very competitive, but I also see the downside. The concepts of the women's movement dovetailed with the way I was. I've always found a lot of male behavior offensive.

"Before I married, I was looking for a strong, assertive woman who'd help me get that competitive monkey off my back. If she was going out there and fighting the world too, it would take some of the weight off me. I met my wife on a blind date and something clicked, but down the road I discovered that she wasn't the feminist I thought she was. Women's rights just aren't an issue for her. I make more money than she does. For all my being on the cutting edge of feminism, I ended up with a woman who has a very traditional job. She's a social worker. There's no money in that, which poses a problem for me. I have to be the traditional male, kicking ass and moving up the ladder, because her small salary doesn't allow me to chill out.

"She's not interested in getting promoted. She works harder than anyone, but when the directorship became available, she didn't want the responsibility. That galled me. We had a couple of big fights. She'd say, 'That's not what I want to do. Why are you trying to make me do something I don't want to do?' My response was, 'Because you're putting all the pressure on me to be on the line.'

"The irony of the situation is that she wants to make me like the kind of macho man that a lot of other women don't want anymore. She wants me to make a whole lot of money. I say to her, 'Do you know what it takes to make a whole lot of money? It takes being away. And once I get into that male mind set about being the breadwinner, that's dangerous. Because the rest of the game is that because I make the money, I get to do anything I want to do. I get to tell you what to do.' I never thought I'd have the kind of wife who encouraged that kind of stuff, but I do. There's a certain kind of woman who can cause her own abuse."

Edgar shook his head and reached for the beer, and something in his face told me he would get nostalgic. "My first girlfriend in college was very smart, very ambitious," he said, his voice getting low, his eyes getting that faraway look. "She's a tenured professor at an Ivy League college. I thought that with her, I could go along for the ride. She wanted an equally successful man." He looked at me and smiled. "There is still a tremendous amount of pressure in this society for men to pump iron."

Dr. Poussaint suggests that men need women to give them permission to move away from the masculine imperative. "If women continue to expect macho, if they come down on men who are trying to change and reject them, the men will go back into being macho."

On the other hand, truly liberated women can certainly inspire men to have what is absolutely essential for their genuine liberation: the desire to change. Robert, 35, a black reporter for a daily newspaper in the Midwest, was a freshman in college in the early seventies when he began his transition from a male chauvinism that was almost misogyny, to the egalitarian human being he says he has become. He credits an affair with a college professor for literally turning his sense of masculinity around. "Up until I met Charlotte I was worse than a traditional male. I used and manipulated women; I didn't respect them at all. I couldn't even call a woman a woman. To me they were all whores or bitches. I felt all women were liars, cheats, no good, and out to get what they could get from a man. I believed most of them traded in on their looks or sexuality to get what they wanted. When I started coming on to my professor, I approached her in the same disrespectful way I approached all women. She disarmed me because she didn't fit any of the stereotypes. We didn't play games. She listened to me tell her all the garbage I believed and she refuted all of it. She was the first woman I met who cared about things, believed in things. She was committed. She was a feminist and that gradually began to rub off on me. Surprisingly, that was very welcome to me.

I'd always disliked dependent women. I always wanted to say to them, 'Can't you handle that?' I was tired of women leaning on me.

"I began to consciously work on myself. It took me six months to stop saying bitch and whore. She never brought it up. I wanted to change. Then I started getting more in touch with my history as a black man. When I started reading, I realized that black women had taken on many roles. We as a people had come through a difficult struggle to get to where we were and it wasn't just because of black men. I guess I began to admire women. What also happened was that Charlotte and I had become friends. She was the first woman friend I'd ever had and ever since that relationship I don't ever want to be with a dependent woman again. I become frustrated with women who don't realize their own potential."

The women's movement had a clear agenda in the early sixties: to help women acquire the economic and political power necessary to improve their lives. What men are charged with lies within their emotional realm. If there is one single act that can remove males from the straitjacket of masculinity, it is learning how to express their emotions and thereby give themselves permission to be human beings, instead of wooden images of strength. They can learn to be more gentle with themselves and other people and even acknowledge their discomfort around women who seem smarter and more powerful than they are.

In a society that denigrates female culture and expression,

anything associated with being female is automatically relegated to a lesser or negative position. The attributes associated with femininity—the ability to nurture, expressiveness, and intuitiveness—are labeled weak and frivolous. In a society where homophobia and misogyny prevail, men can easily be controlled and prevented from expressing the full range of human emotions, including "feminine" ones out of fear of being labeled homosexual or weak. As men learn to value female culture, they can begin to confront the paralyzing fear of expressing their feminine side. "When I began to have women as friends, I learned there was a whole new way of viewing life," said one man. "Women handle a lot of things better than men. They handle money better. I actually believe I'll never have anything materially unless I get married. I know a lot of single women who own their own homes, cars, and take nice vacations. They're better managers."

"Part of the issue is that what women do has always been defined as not strong," said Dr. Poussaint. "That was propaganda. A lot of macho men are very dependent on their wives. These men don't know how to do the daily routines of living. They can't wash their own clothes, cook their own food, or keep the house clean. They've assigned these activities to women. The macho man was allowed to be the person with wisdom about the outside world, but men have always delegated a lot to women. It's obvious men think women have some skills."

There are male and female traits in all human beings. As

women must learn the skills of achieving power in the larger world, men must explore femininity within themselves and use it to improve their lives. "Men need to let themselves feel more dependent and not be scared of that. They need to let themselves be taken care of more," suggested Dr. Poussaint. "Men would benefit from more intimacy. They need to learn how to trust other men."

According to Herb Goldberg, in his books *The New Male* and *The New Male-Female Relationship*, males have been coerced into duplicating an image of stoic masculinity in order to control the opposite sex. In the same way, women have been tricked into duplicating an image of passive dependency in order to attract and manipulate men. These images have given us men who fear weakness, failure, and dependence and women who fear success, power, and independence. Definitions of male success can be expanded to include cooperation and interdependence as well as competition and control. This isn't to say that men would no longer be ambitious or driven, but that that is not all they could be. They would be able to express themselves in a lot more ways than society now allows them. The new men's movement has to make room for men who love independence for themselves and for the women in their lives.

To minimize the sexism within each partner, both have to recognize that their actions don't occur in a sexual vacuum. Goldberg points out that behavior in one partner depends on a counterpart response in the other partner. Men and women can minimize the sexism in their partner by changing their own behavior that encourages the other person's sexism. In the past women sought to stifle the sexism of males by appealing to their sense of fair play and, failing that, their guilt. The kind of change that comes from being intimidated or shamed is usually short-lived. Backlash is the end product when change is forced on people who aren't emotionally ready for it. When partners create a climate of open communication and tolerance for self-expression, they usually grow as a couple.

There are very few men or women who have grown up in homes where they witnessed true sexual equality and tolerance. Most of us share childhoods rooted in sexism, which is why it was necessary for the women's movement to be buttressed by the consciousness-raising sessions and support groups of networking women striving for freer lives. Men who begin to claim their own movement must begin to set in place similar supports for liberation. By associating with men who also want to change and give expression to their softer side and aligning themselves with men who are open as well as competitive, men form supportive friendships. These contribute to the kind of masculinity that isn't affronted by independent women, but rather finds them allies in a human movement for positive change. Robert says that after he became more egalitarian, many of his friendships with more traditional men went by the wayside. "I grew past them," he says simply.

By choosing for companions women who also want to develop as independent human beings, men further their own growth. Clinging, dependent women who use their sexuality to manipulate men don't support the new masculine movement. They have too much to lose. Angry women who use the women's movement as an excuse to express their hatred for all men denigrate, rather than support sincere change in men. The partner for a man seeking change is a woman heading in the same direction toward a life that tried to free itself of sexist limitations. And if he wants support for his own new life-style, he will have to support the growth of the woman he cares for. "I have a woman friend," said Oscar, 32, a manager for a large pharmaceutical company, "who is really smart and hardworking. She was working in an office doing a job two steps above her pay grade and promotion level. She was doing all of the work and not getting the title or the money. She needed to go to school and we spent a lot of time talking about what to do. We strategized. She got a promotion. She got a raise. She got a scholarship. I helped her discover the courage she needed to go after those things."

He says he is getting a lot from the relationship. "She's a hell of a lot better at ten million things than I am. I'm getting emotional growth out of the relationship."

Oscar says his sex life has improved since he doesn't feel compelled to always be the one to initiate and perform. He enjoys pleasing his woman, but no longer accepts the total responsibility for providing her pleasure. When men are no longer forced to perform in bed, they find they can relax and enjoy tenderness for the first time.

Whether men have benefit of counseling, are assisted in

their struggle by women, or embark on self-discovery and development alone, they will need to be patient with themselves. Going against the grain is a lonely business, but refusing to change with the times is worse. The fifties are gone and won't be coming back again. Women are happier being able to fulfill their promise than they were being forced to live according to society's dictates. No one is advocating the death of the macho man, rather the integration of the traditional man with other components of personhood. Men can either begin the journey of self-introspection that leads to growth and more harmonious relationships with women, or they can cling to images and myths that ultimately destroy their marriages and even their lives. The rewards for expanding their vision of themselves are there for the taking.

12

Let's Be Friends

Between the years 1980 and 1983, my circle of divorced women friends expanded greatly. We banded together out of economic and emotional necessity. We babysat for each other's children, loaned each other money, food, our cars, and, most important of all, we listened to each other talk, moan, and cry. We were all in varying stages of culture shock. The ink wasn't yet dry on our divorce papers but we had bills to pay, children to rear, and already, the support payments weren't coming. Our battle scars weren't healing; they were still oozing. We were, for the most part, still very bitter toward our ex-husbands and not very hopeful about our future with men. Yet, more than anything, we longed for the security of a committed relationship.

We loved talking about men, loved dissecting and analyzing their behavior. Thumbs up if they supported our professional ambitions, our aggressive and assertive tendencies. Thumbs down if they mentioned a fondness for home-cooked meals, the smell of sun-dried wash, an after-work martini served by soft, feminine hands. We would have none of that. We wouldn't tolerate a repeat of the backlash of our first marriages. This time we knew better. We would find men who liked and respected women, men secure enough to feel proud of our success. We would lay our cards on the table, discuss our professional aspirations up front so there would be no misunderstanding. If a man could deal with an ambitious woman, fine. If not, we'd be moving on. The second time around was going to be different. We were going to find Mr. Liberated Goodbar. With nuts.

The perfect man was, according to most of my friends: egalitarian, professional, ambitious, intelligent, handsome, crazy about our children, and earning enough money to restore to us a semblance of the good life we'd forfeited by getting divorces. (While we didn't want to be desired solely as sex objects, we had no qualms about viewing men as economic objects.) Initially none of us had any difficulty locating the perfect guy. I'd get a call at some crazy time of day or night and it would be Tina or Lesley or Rachel, rhapsodizing about some new lover's superior qualities and wanting to know if her child could spend the weekend at my house. The problems arose within a short time, when my friend would have discovered he was: a. not divorced yet;

b. couldn't cope with her ambition, her superior earnings, her lack of domesticity; c. didn't want to get married; d. all of the above.

Our steadiest dates were with each other. "It's so unfair," we cried, as the first and second years of our independence spun past us. Our ex-husbands were all married, or living with someone, or happily screwing everything that moved, and we were alone: "A man can get any kind of woman he wants. If he wants a career woman, she's available. If he wants a stay-at-home wife, she's available. A guy can even get someone who'll let him stay home. But where is the man to fill our needs? They're all such dogs."

Some of us, of course, managed to find the proverbial good guy. In fact, several women encountered men who were quite strong in their desire for an equal relationship. These men raised my girlfriends' feminist consciousness and insisted that women hold up their end of the fifty-fifty. One friend told me how her liberated boyfriend became angry when after driving them both to a concert and parking her car in a lot, she couldn't locate it after the concert had ended. "He accused me of depending on him to find the car just because he's the man. And he was right," she admitted.

I recall going out to a disco with Jessica and her live-in lover, Bill. Before we left their apartment, Bill became angry when he discovered that Jessica and I were about to go out without any money. "How is it that you women work, make just as much money as I do, and yet you still expect me to pay for everything because I'm the man?" he asked sarcastically. Neither my friend nor I had an answer.

Despite the exceptions, however, there didn't seem to be enough liberated men to go around. We were lonely. And as time passed and our dates thinned out, that loneliness turned to a desperation that eroded our resolve. One by one, we chose the best of what was available and settled for movies and dinner, for someone who could fix our cars and discipline our sons, for affection. And in return most of our boyfriends wanted what we'd just escaped: that we be dependent, subservient, second. It was really quite amazing how quickly we accepted again what we'd just gotten out of. We sighed and cooked our new men dinner and cleared a space in our homes so that they could do their very important work while we cleaned up the kitchen. We gave them the extra time we needed to advance our careers, fulfill our dreams. And when they asked us to let our hair and fingernails grow longer, to lose five pounds and wear more fashionable clothes, we obliged and began to spend more time on our hair, clothes, and fingernails than we did on our goals.

I let a man have that effect on me until my own weakness made me angry. "Listen, buddy," I'd say into the bathroom mirror, "I have some important things to do with my life. I like you very much, but you just can't have all my time, all my energy, all my creativity." I was very bold in front of a mirror, but outside the bathroom I was drifting toward becoming the woman I vowed I didn't want to be. I couldn't deny that my commitment and resolve to pursue my goals were being eroded by my succumbing to my new boyfriend's

very silent demands. And I couldn't deny the growing sus-
picion that his demands were designed to do just that. This
was déjà vu of the worst kind. Why had I let myself become
so dependent on pleasing him? He wasn't all that wonderful.
Hell, he wasn't as wonderful as I.

The irony of my situation and that of my other women
friends didn't strike me then with the clarity that would
come later: we felt as powerless out of our marriages as we
had in them. It hadn't dawned on us that if we were paying
our bills and rearing our children without much support,
something very few men we knew were doing, then we were
strong enough to take control of our own lives and find men
who could give us more of what we wanted. What was
frightening was that we seemed resigned to a vicious, self-
defeating cycle of deferring to the wishes of men in order to
keep them in our lives, then hating ourselves for being weak.

Overwhelmed by that realization, frightened of who I was
becoming, I chopped off practically all my hair in a spon-
taneous act of revolution. It ended up not being the bold
step to recapture my independence that I'd envisioned. After
I left the barbershop, I had a relapse. I lost my nerve and
spent the rest of my time with my boyfriend (not long
enough for my hair to grow back) worrying that he might
not like me with short hair.

We broke up anyway. In the aftermath, I found myself
without a man and, after my fear of loneliness wore off, very
relieved at the prospect of having so much time for me. I
took out a dusty manuscript, bought six legal pads, and

booked a flight to California for a working vacation at a friend's home. And there, with my mind solidly on my work, my belief in my own abilities slowly returning, with wild short hair and raggedy fingernails, I met Mr. Right and began a relationship that was to become essential to my new life.

I discovered during my vacation and in the long-distance romance that ensued that Ellis cooked, he cleaned, he gave me space. He bragged about my work and meant it. He didn't seem to care if I knew more about something than he did and would listen to my explanations. He helped me mother my child. He sympathized when I complained about deadlines and offered sensible advice. He wouldn't allow me to wallow in depression. He demanded that I be an adult most of the time, but was comforting when I needed him to be. He seemed to understand and respect my need for an equal relationship and told me that's what he wanted too. He was, in a word, wonderful. And I didn't for one minute trust it would last.

"Listen," I said before I agreed to a wedding, "let's get something very straight. Don't think because I work out of the house that I'll be available for drudgery duty. I'm not going to the cleaners to drop your shirts off or pick them up. I'm not going to run your little errands. I'm not going to do all the cleaning and cooking. When I have a deadline I will stay up all night long and get it out. If people recognize me for my work, I'm going to enjoy it. I want to retain my name for professional reasons. . . ." On and on I droned with my list of what I wanted, what I demanded in our marriage. Ellis was somewhat taken aback, but he listened, asked questions, negotiated some things and agreed to others. Ellis, of course, had his own needs and he shared those with me. And after we had thoroughly reviewed all the cards on the table we got married.

It is difficult to analyze what makes some men go against the grain of a male-dominated society and choose to make their marriages egalitarian. When so many men feel threatened by female independence it is difficult to conceive of men who voluntarily yield power. Yet, it is apparent some husbands have created a new masculine value system that has as its foundation support for women's rights. These men don't view themselves as giving up anything. They may be conscious that their behavior sets them apart from their peers, but that doesn't cause them to feel uncomfortable or on the losing end of the marital stick. In fact, what most of the male interviewees I judged to be truly egalitarian said to me is that they couldn't understand why the majority of men continued to function in accordance to a sexist behavioral code. They didn't consider the subservience that sexist men gleamed from their wives as a benefit. They considered themselves more content than their chauvinistic peers and believed their marriages were more stable.

They certainly appeared a lot happier to me. As I interviewed dual-career couples across the country, I began to spot quite easily the marriages where there was true equality. Unlike the tension of the couples caught up in backlash, the men and women who were attempting to live as equals were relaxed with each other and engrossed with communicating. As I sat across from them in their living rooms and in restaurants, they most often talked with each other, more than with me. They used me as a sort of a facilitator, assisting them in exploring and enjoying each other more. They raised their voices and argued passionately, cutting each other off, challenging their partner's statements, teasing, laughing, and visibly loving. These couples seemed at once ambitious and willing to defer to the other's ambition if that need arose. There was a tremendous amount of trust; they didn't expect their vulnerabilities to be used against them. Many of the men attributed the genesis of their open spirit to their wives.

I remember sitting with a thoroughly delightful couple in a dimly lit Philadelphia restaurant for hours, feeling as if I had been invited to an intimate soirée. Married for seven years, Jeanne and Kirk seemed like complete opposites. He was a quiet, thoughtful WASP, with the good looks of a movie star. Jeanne was the rounded, raven-haired epitome of Jewish chutzpah and guilt, cutting off her husband to get her point across one minute, then apologizing in the next for monopolizing the conversation. They always looked each other in the eye when they spoke and they smiled often. They both worked in advertising, and for a time had worked for the same company. Kirk had proudly told me that Jeanne had been the first female department head at her company. He said that he'd always liked and respected women, but that Jeanne had made him comfortable with a new masculine value system. She had released him from a macho mode that had begun to chafe him.

"One night, there were three people in the office working very late—Kirk, another friend, and me," said Jeanne. "We'd finished the project and Kirk and I were playing backgammon and he kept losing. He was very frightened and frustrated. I said, 'What's your problem?' And he said, 'I don't like losing.' And I replied, 'What's the difference as long as you had fun?' "

For Kirk, the question was a revelation. "I think men are taught to be performance-oriented and to win. Her statement was revolutionary. I thought, in the game of life this is the woman I want by my side. There was extreme comfort and security in that statement." The security of their relationship engenders trust and something that was completely lacking in backlash relationships: a willingness to obey each other, sometimes even without question.

When Jeanne, Kirk, and I had completed dinner, they offered to drive me to my next interview. As we approached my destination, they recognized the home as that of friends of theirs. Kirk was pleased that he and his friends were sharing the same experience and in his enthusiasm, almost raced to the front door of the house so that he could say hello. It was an awkward situation, since I had promised all of my interviewees anonymity. Jeanne perceived my position immediately and called Kirk back to their car. "It's supposed to be anonymous, honey," she reminded her husband. He looked at her blankly, then nodded his understanding. "Right," he said, turning away from the door.

It wasn't surprising to discover that egalitarian couples seemed to get a lot more satisfaction and joy out of their children than couples for whom childcare is the subject of arguments and hostility. In the most successful dual-career couples where the husband is truly participating, both mothers and fathers seem to consider themselves equal parents and are extremely child-centered. One of the most vivid examples of this occurred in the home of a suburban Pittsburgh couple. Nathan and JoAnn were both in public relations and had a one-year-old daughter. They'd planned for my visit and had asked a friend to come over to occupy their daughter while we talked. As the interview was coming to a close, I heard the soft babbling of a young toddler. Our conversation instantly ceased and I watched in delight as the mother and father submitted to being mesmerized by their own child. They both wanted to hold her, but the toddler clamored for her father's arms. "She's a daddy's girl," JoAnn told me, chuckling softly. "At night, sometimes we fight to see who gets a chance to bathe her," said Nathan.

Tom and Leah were another example of a child-centered couple. Their system of mutual childcare was so entrenched, either partner seemed to automatically care for their daughter when the other was busy. While Leah answered my questions, Tom stroked his eleven-year-old's hair, as she snuggled close to him on the sofa.

Though I looked, I could find no pattern in determining which men would achieve an equal relationship with their wives. When I interviewed a couple in Washington, the man, a medical researcher, told me he'd been brought up in a single family household with a working mother. Aha! I thought. But Kirk grew up in a traditional home, with a mother who stayed at home. The writer said he adored his mother. Tom thought his Italian immigrant mother was a fool and a doormat and declared he had stopped listening to her when he was nine. A professional musician recalled that his full-time homemaker mother taught him and his brother how to cook, sew, iron, wash dishes and clothes, chores they were expected to perform. A lawyer, who values his wife's independence, declared he was waited on hand and foot by his mother who worked full-time. One thing most agreed upon: the women's movement hadn't been the catalyst for their new value system. "The women's movement had no impact on me," said Tom. "I'd already gone beyond what they wanted." "I don't think feminism had a really big impact. Basically, I think I was already there. I might have needed some fine tuning," said a writer from Chicago.

I'm not sure the women's movement had as little impact on egalitarian men as these men suggest. At the very least, that movement probably crystallized some concepts for them and served as a strong motivating influence, a kind of societal thrust toward equality. At the most, it galvanized their consciences and prodded them to change their behavior toward women. The women's movement probably made them feel less isolated and thus increased their chances of sustaining an equal relationship. But I agree that the women's movement, or, for that matter, a man's childhood or mother, have less to do with his being egalitarian than another factor: Men who want equal relationships are men who value women as friends. *It is the firm foundation of friendship that precludes backlash.*

That was the thread I'd been looking for, and the men I interviewed enthusiastically admitted their wives were their best friends. Kirk told me, "Jeanne and I are a corporation. I respect and like women. I don't think most men do. The best thing about being married to Jeanne is that I constantly learn emotionally, intellectually, and physically." "Over the years we've become better and better friends," said a writer from Washington, D.C. "I don't really have any men friends. She is the person I feel closest to in this world. We share a lot." A scientist from Baltimore told me, "I hope I'm encouraging my wife's success. I think it's great she's a doctor. I want her to be happy. I don't want to be stuck with an unhappy woman for the rest of my life. I like smart women. My wife is my best buddy." "We started off as very good friends," said Nathan. "I knew my wife had the personality to be a worker. I encouraged it selfishly. Two incomes are better than one and I want her to be fulfilled." It is the belief that each partner's success translates ultimately into the success of the couple that underscores the friendship these men and women share.

It is my own friendship with my husband that is the glue in our relationship. It's what's enabled us to survive the changes in our marriage, for, despite my grand pronouncements, Ellis did change. So did I. Before we'd been married two years, we'd fallen into some of the usual gender-influenced patterns. And yet, I don't feel oppressed by cooking, which I do most of, annoyed occasionally, but not boxed into a corner I hate.

In two-career marriages that work, there is a little elbow room, space for when the patterns get too constricting. When he doesn't feel like doing the long-distance driving, she takes the wheel. When she gets tired of cooking, he has to get something on the table. Such couples rarely fight about role division and if they do, they aren't battles of the sexes. They are fights about washing dishes and emptying the trash, not about power. He's not first; she's not last. There is no backlash.

There is, of course, a lot of luck involved in meeting "the right person," especially when that means a man with egalitarian tendencies. But, in some respects, we make our own luck. One liberated husband confessed that he might "misuse" a weak woman. "I wouldn't want to," he explained, "but if you are with someone who lets you get away with whatever, the average person is just going to take advantage of that."

Fifty-fifty marriages, where husband and wife are friends, seem to endure largely because the wives recognize and exercise their own strength. True friendship can only exist between equals. The women who empower and affirm themselves are the women who don't have backlash in their marriages. "You have to know what you're worth," my friend Ruth once told me. She had married Jim, a man I'd known when he was another friend's husband. His first marriage to a quiet, passive woman had been troubled and that wife complained that Jim didn't share in household chores. Jim seemed to be a somewhat overbearing, macho man, intent on making his wife bend to his will. Hindsight tells me his attitude may have been shaped by his wife's passivity and dependence. "He didn't respect her," was Ruth's succinct comment when we talked about her husband's first wife. I was amazed that Jim and Ruth had such an equal marriage; they shared chores and decision making. Rather than attempting to suppress her, Jim seemed proud of his wife and boasted about her success and how she helped him accomplish his goals. Part of the change I saw in Jim was probably a factor of age, and some, of course, was due to his previous marital experience and the influence of the women's movement. But I think more had to do with Ruth. "I noticed early on when Jim and I got into arguments, if I backed down or acted weak, he'd take advantage of me. So now I don't back down." Ruth's first husband had been intimidated by her success as an independent businesswoman and the experience of backlash had reaffirmed her resolve to be strong, even if it meant being alone. "I have told him before if certain things don't happen, we'll just have to part."

"I prefer being alone to being with someone awful," said a divorced mother of three teenaged children. "That's not to say that being alone can't be pretty damn hard. I've had some really miserable holiday blues at times, but it wasn't as depressing as being in a marriage where you're not a person. I don't do too badly alone. Women just have to know they are strong. We are very strong. We can do it alone if we have to. It all boils down to believing in yourself."

In the midst of this bleak landscape there are a few hopeful signs. Some male and female workers are pushing institutions to deal with reconciling the home and work lives of the nation's families.

The United States is the only modern industrialized country without federal policies concerning maternity, childcare, and daycare. And yet, according to the Bureau of Labor Statistics in 1998, 71.8 percent of all mothers worked, and 77.9 percent of working women had children between the ages of 6–17. Many of these women are married but if neither mother nor father is able to take time off to care for newborns, the entire family is placed in financial and emotional jeopardy.

The prevailing belief is that women who have children aren't committed to their jobs, but according to an extensive study of corporate parental leave policies conducted by Catalyst, a national nonprofit organization, women are interested in both careers and family. They do not want to stay away from their jobs for an extended period of time. Polling 384 corporations and 112 women, the Catalyst study found that women deemed the ideal maternity leave period to be only three months but new mothers did want to be paid during their leave as well as during a part-time transition back onto the job.

The Pregnancy Discrimination Act passed in 1978 required employers to treat pregnancy as a short-term disability. Catalyst's report showed that 95 percent of the companies they interviewed offered some leave. Only 38.9 percent offered full payment with disability leave, while 57.3 percent offered partial payment and 3.8 percent provided no payment at all. Although 37 percent offered unpaid leave to men, the company attitude clashed with their own policy in many cases. Of those offering maternity leave to men, 41 percent didn't consider it reasonable for them to take it.

Beyond the issue of maternity leave loom other problems that demand federal intervention. Federal intervention might encourage more employers to offer flex time, job sharing, sick leave to care for ill children, and the choice of working at home when possible.

While not all issues are easy to pinpoint, sexism in the workplace is clearly a double-edged sword that wounds men and women. Female power is still linked to the amount of money women earn at their jobs. In Asia, for example, women in Bangladesh earn as little as 42 percent of what men earn. Women in the Syrian Arab Republic earn only 60 percent of what men earn . . . Chile's women earn 61 percent of what men earn. In Japan, about 37 percent of working women hold low-wage jobs—compared with only 6 percent of men. In the United States, about 33 percent of working women hold low-wage jobs—compared with 20 percent of men. In France, 25 percent of working women hold low-wage jobs—compared with 13 percent of men. Worldwide, women hold only 14 percent of administrative and managerial jobs and less than 6 percent of senior management jobs.[24] When women earn substantially less than men and their access to advancement is stymied because of discrimination, there is a tendency to make up for the lack of economic worth by being more subservient. The lower earning potential of their mates hampers men from breaking out of the macho breadwinner mold—and all the traditional expectations that accompany that mind set. Corporate sexism imperils the survival of American families. And it endangers big business. In a workforce that is increasingly female, sexism and lack of sensitivity for female culture could cause morale problems that might ultimately affect the bottom line.

Beyond the issues of equal pay for equal work, federally funded daycare, maternity and paternity leave, and job sharing, is the pressing issue of female self-empowerment. Legislation alone cannot achieve that; the battle also must be won within the psyches of women and men who wish to live happily together.

The solution to backlash isn't for women to become less ambitious or successful, but for them to claim their own power and honestly communicate their needs to their husbands, believing those needs can be met, prepared to take action if they are not. The friendship men and women need

---

[24] From "Who's Minding Our Pre-Schoolers?" March 1996, based on 1993 Census Bureau info.

in their marriages can only take place between two equally powerful beings. There can be no friendship if, out of the same fear of abandonment, the woman allows herself to be intimidated and the man allows himself to become a psychic bully. Self-empowerment for women will be a slow evolution, one that won't be complete until a whole generation of women and men are comfortable with female strength and begin passing on that comfort to their sons and daughters. Backlash will continue to burden dual-career couples until men and women begin to recognize female power and male self-realization as the forces that can end their fears and solidify their friendship.